BEHIND THE GATES OF GOMORRAH

BEHIND THE GATES OF GOMORRAH

Life inside one of America's largest hospitals for the criminally insane, treating the real Hannibal Lecters of this world

STEPHEN SEAGER

ALLEN&UNWIN
SYDNEY • MELBOURNE • AUCKLAND • LONDON

This edition published in 2018
First published in Australia and New Zealand by Allen & Unwin in 2015
First published in the United States in 2014 by Gallery Books,
a division of Simon & Schuster, Inc.

Allen & Unwin
83 Alexander Street
Crows Nest NSW 2065
Australia
Phone: (61 2) 8425 0100
Email: info@allenandunwin.com
Web: www.allenandunwin.com

Cataloguing-in-Publication details are available
from the National Library of Australia
www.trove.nla.gov.au

ISBN 978 1 76063 236 6

Internal design by Jaime Putorti and Luke Causby
Printed and bound in Australia by SOS Print + Media

10 9 8 7 6 5

MIX
Paper from
responsible sources
FSC® C011217
FSC
www.fsc.org

The paper in this book is FSC® certified.
FSC® promotes environmentally responsible,
socially beneficial and economically viable
management of the world's forests.

For the victims,
and their families.

For the staff,
and their families.

For the patients,
and their families.

And He will wipe away every tear from their eyes . . .

there will no longer be any mourning, or crying, or pain . . .

—Revelations 21:4

AUTHOR'S NOTE

For reasons both of patient confidentiality and consideration of my coworkers, the only real name I use in this account is my own. I have also changed the specifics of the events recounted so that they do not identify the participants. What I have not changed is the essential reality of the events that I experienced or witnessed.

A forensic state mental hospital is, by its very nature, a distilled environment. While the vast majority of persons suffering with mental illness are not criminals or violent, the majority of persons referred to forensic hospitals are or have been such.

A forensic state mental hospital is not a safe place. I have nothing but admiration for the staff who perform their jobs in the face of great adversity. And, never losing sight of the suffering of their victims, I have respect for the forensic state mental hospital patients who live under even greater duress.

Everyone asks me why Napa State Hospital has to be such a violent, dangerous, yet persistently unguarded place. The answer holds today, as it did on my first day at Gomorrah: you can't be a hospital and a prison at the same time.

• • •

THE PATIENT RIGHTS system and current mental-health laws, both well-intentioned, conspire to make a system in which the rights of the patients are paramount and often detrimental to the staff and other patients' safety. Since the 1960s and '70s, forensic mental hospitals have suffered from the effects of the anti-psychiatry movement. The basic tenet of this philosophy says that mental illness isn't truly a disease but a reaction to the trauma or damage that modern society inflicts on persons. It supposes that psychiatric treatment—read medications—does more harm than good and openly states that psychiatric hospitals are just jails for punishing those who defy arbitrary societal norms. And it concludes that if racism, poverty, injustice, and inequality (and psychiatry) could be overcome, mental illness would disappear.

While modern medical science has now proven the opposite to be true, that the major mental disorders are truly structural diseases of the brain just as heart diseases are structural diseases of the heart, there remain in high government and hospital positions persons steeped in this erroneous anti-psychiatry paradigm and its residue continues to influence both state and national policy.

Psychiatrists share in the blame for this problem as well. We allowed the anti-psychiatry movement to go largely unchallenged. Some of us wholeheartedly participated. We stood by while state hospitals were emptied and our patients were flung into the streets. Now wringing our hands and bemoaning the fates, we tolerate the epidemic violence inflicted on our new forensic patients in places like Napa State, which propagate and tolerate legally sanctioned mistreatment of the very persons we are ethically charged to defend.

PREFACE

Raymond Boudreaux and I sat at opposite ends of a rickety wooden table—with him nearest to the door. This was a mistake.

Two fluorescent ceiling tubes lit the cramped space, and the walls were war-surplus beige. A single small window in the door looked out into a hallway.

The July air hung musty and still. My chair made a tiny screech against the chipped linoleum floor as I slid it forward.

"Mr. Boudreaux, good afternoon," I said. "I'm Dr. Seager."

Boudreaux didn't reply. Clad in robin's-egg-blue hospital scrubs, he was a hulking black man with shoulders wide as goalposts. I felt fixed in his gaze.

"Mr. Boudreaux . . . ?" I tried again. Boudreaux's eyes didn't waver. I shifted uncomfortably, wondering how long someone could actually go without blinking.

A psychiatrist, I'd recently been hired to run an inpatient unit at a large state forensic mental hospital. It was the kind of dangerous, unsettling place made familiar by the fictitious Baltimore State in *The Silence of the Lambs*. After a week of training, Raymond Boudreaux was the first patient I'd talked to alone. I was rushing to get home. It was late, and the room had been convenient.

"I'm your new doctor," I persisted. "How are you feeling, sir?"

Another pause. Then Boudreaux's impassive face changed. "You're a bloodsucker, aren't you?" He smiled, his Creole-tinged voice smooth as glass. He tipped his head and studied me like a curious dog. His eyes narrowed. My heart leaped.

A forensic mental hospital isn't like a regular mental hospital. The patients aren't just psychotic. They're also criminals. They're the school shooters, James Holmeses, and Jeffrey Dahmers of the world. I'd seen Raymond Boudreaux on CNN when he was first arrested.

Boudreaux's breathing accelerated. "You and that fucking district attorney," he said. "You're both in this together. I know your kind. You'll beat a man to death, then suck the blood out of his corpse."

Boudreaux, a New Orleans native, had graduated from Yale with an MBA. He'd worked in management for a bank in San Francisco. Then he became ill. A month after his termination, he killed his boss and several coworkers with a shotgun.

"I'm going to strangle that faggot DA," Boudreaux snarled as he stood. "Or you." His massive frame partially obscured the door and I became acutely aware of the seating error. Panicked, I stood as well.

With hands as large as skillets, Boudreaux grabbed the edges of the table and pushed it forward, pinning my thighs to the wall. My chair clattered to the floor. I looked frantically toward the small window into the hallway but saw nothing. I reached for the belt alarm we'd been issued for situations like this and remembered that it was still in my office.

Sweat rolled off the crest of Boudreaux's shaven head. "Don't move, you son of a bitch," he seethed, and pushed the table harder.

Amid the terrified jumble in my head, an old piece of advice appeared: "If you're ever cornered by an angry patient," a medical school instructor had once told me, "keep talking."

"Tell me about your crime."

The veins in Boudreaux's neck bulged and his eyes widened. The table hit bone in my legs. He took a couple of choppy breaths, and then the pressure on my legs waned. Boudreaux's head dropped and his stare softened.

He let go of the table, sat back down, and put a hand on his forehead. He looked smaller. He looked mortal.

"I killed my closest friends," Boudreaux said slowly. "What kind of a person does that?"

I edged out from behind the table.

"A person with an illness does that," I said, sidling toward the door. I reached around a slumped Boudreaux and grabbed the door handle. "That's why you're here and not in prison. You're not bad, you're sick."

Opening the door, I glanced down the long hallway and hurriedly waved toward Lola Palanqui, a unit nurse, and two strapping psych techs, who hustled toward me. My legs began to tremble, but I managed to turn back to Boudreaux.

"Will you be okay?"

Boudreaux said nothing.

"The staff will help you back to your room," I said, and stumbled aside as the cavalry arrived.

The two techs escorted Boudreaux back down the hall.

Dark hair, thirties, Palanqui stood before me with her hands on her hips. We were nearly toe-to-toe. For the second time, I'd been backed against a wall. Although I grimaced in pain, she glared up at me.

"Were you in there alone with Mr. Boudreaux?" Palanqui asked in Tagalog-accented English.

"Yes . . ."

"Didn't they tell you not to do that?"

"Yes . . ."

"He could have killed you."

I caught a breath. "I know. It was really fright—"

"Didn't you learn anything from that terrible first day?" she said.

I touched the stitches in the back of my head. "I just thought . . ." I didn't know what to say.

"We need you, Doc," Palanqui said, and touched my arm. "Please get smarter."

I sank to the floor. I'd taken the state hospital job thinking I could help. But I was on my way to getting myself or someone else killed.

Boudreaux called from the end of the hallway. He was walking to dinner with the rest of the patients.

"Thanks, Doc," he said with a wave.

BEHIND THE GATES OF GOMORRAH

CHAPTER ONE

Mad Hatter: "Why is a raven like a writing-desk?" . . .

"Have you guessed the riddle yet?" the Hatter said, turning to Alice again.

"No, I give it up," Alice replied: "what's the answer?"

"I haven't the slightest idea," said the Hatter.

—Lewis Carroll, *Alice's Adventures in Wonderland*

I arrived early for my first day of work. A remnant of centuries past, Napa State Hospital spreads over hundreds of acres in a remote valley corner, hidden from view.

Pulling onto an unobtrusive access road, I connected to Magnolia Lane, a long main drive bracketed by rows of enormous spreading elms and ornate nineteenth-century mansions. I'd just spent a full week of orientation in one of them. I recalled a lecture on the hospital's history.

In 1872 a site was selected and work began for the creation of Napa State Hospital, one of America's largest forensic psychiatric institutions, and one of California's first hospitals dedicated solely to the care of the chronically insane. The doors opened November 15, 1875. From then until 1954, when the facility underwent a complete renovation, the hospital and its surrounding environs were a self-sufficient community. In 1992, with the erection of the safety fence, Napa State Hospital became a fully accredited forensic psychiatric facility and began accepting mentally ill patients remanded by the statewide criminal justice system.

We'd been given a handout that contained the Napa State Hospital "mission statement." It read "We promote a safe, secure, non-coercive/violence-free environment for patients served, staff, visitors, and the community."

I turned right onto Spruce Lane, which swung by a newer administration building with a cluster of Spanish-style stucco structures behind it. These back buildings contained the "open" psychiatric units at Napa, which I'd toured during orientation. They mostly housed the older, more debilitated patients, who can come and go pretty much as they please. On a patch of lawn, I saw a group of slouched men quietly smoking cigarettes; two leaned on walkers.

"Won't they just escape?" someone asked our instructor when we'd seen a similar crew during orientation.

"Where would they go?"

My initial appointment had been to Unit Twelve, one of these open units, until two days before, when I received a call from Dr. Heidi Francis, the Napa State medical director.

"There's been a switch in your assignment," Dr. Francis said. "You'll be going to Unit C."

"What's Unit C?" I asked.

"I'll email you a map," she replied.

I parked in a crowded lot striped with faded paint. Pausing

beside my red Toyota truck, I clipped a new orange security badge to the front pocket of my shirt and straightened my tie.

During my tenure in the mental health world, I'd been employed at many different psychiatric hospitals, but I'd never worked in a state forensic facility.

Walking slowly toward Unit C, I approached the towering "safety" fence, extending as far as one could see. The chain-link barrier stood twenty feet high. A three-foot continuous coil of razor wire ran along the top. The fence enclosed Napa State's secure treatment area, or STA, which contained the hospital's seventeen high-risk locked units. No one stood outside smoking here. Police cars patrolled the main drives. The compound looked like a sprawling prisoner-of-war camp in a World War II movie. The STA, our orientation instructor had said, housed the hospital's "bad actors." New hires weren't supposed to be assigned "inside the fence," so I hadn't worried much about it.

I moved toward a tall gate, which suddenly buzzed loudly. Standing beside me, an older gentleman eased the stile open and we stepped inside a monitored entryway. He closed the gate and I startled when it locked with a decisive snap.

"First day?" the other man asked.

"Yes it is," I replied. "I've never really been in—" Before I could finish, the older man pointed to my badge and we both ran our employee IDs through a reader. His name tag read "R. Corcoran." From behind a thick glass partition, uniformed men inspected our data on a huge computer screen. As we waited, Corcoran touched my tie and shook his head. He made a fist beside his neck and raised his hand, pretending to hang himself. I whisked off the tie and jammed it into my pants pocket.

A second gate opened, behind which another pod and two new officers awaited.

"Arms up," a compact Filipino cop said. His badge read "Bangban." He waved a handheld sensor coil up and around my body.

"What time does the flight leave?" I said, but no one laughed.

"Pockets," the second officer said. I removed the necktie, keys, coins, and pens from my pants pockets and dropped them into a plastic tray. Bangban eyed the tie and smirked.

"This whole business is called a sally port," Corcoran said as we collected our loose items. I rolled up my tie and returned it to my pocket. We slipped our shoes back on.

"*Sally port* sounds so benign," I said.

"They're used at maximum-security prisons, like San Quentin," Corcoran continued. "The U.S. Mints and nuclear missile installations."

We entered a third inspection area. Standing in front of a thick tinted-glass window, I saw another clump of dimly lit policemen on the other side.

"That's where they strip-search you," Corcoran said, nodding toward the darkened pane. "Or explore a body cavity."

Mouth dry, I glanced at the window. "Who gets searched?" I said, but Corcoran was already in front of the final gate. It hummed and we exited onto the hospital grounds.

I followed Corcoran to a final window where I was issued my hospital keys and a "personal alarm" to wear on my belt. Atop the alarm was a red button that was to be activated, we were told during orientation, in case of any "trouble."

The Napa State STA doesn't fit a traditional hospital mold. A collection of one- and two-story buildings lies in an expansive arc, like pearls on an enormous string, enfolded by the ubiquitous fence. Redone in 1954, the units echo the classic elongated ranch-style models from that era.

Each structure had been freshly painted and was well maintained. Neatly trimmed old-growth trees dotted the scene. Through it all ran an ocean of mown grass. Inside the fence, the STA looked like a college campus.

Amid this verdant set piece, peacocks strutted and preened in the sun. A shimmering blue bird perched atop a cinder-block wall lifted his head and trumpeted. His call rang out in two parts, both eerily human. The first sounded like a staccato burst of laughter, the second like a person screaming for help.

As I stepped into the main building that housed Unit C, an ear-splitting siren blared suddenly and a dozen strobes flashed. From doorways that lined a long corridor, people emerged at a run and began searching frantically. Some shouted. "Is everybody okay?" a large man yelled.

"Check the dining hall," a young woman exclaimed, waving to her left, and a dozen persons surged in that direction. And still the siren wailed and lights flashed.

I stood paralyzed. To my right a casually dressed, fortyish woman with short brown hair glanced at me. She fingered my ID badge.

"Are you the new doctor?" she shouted above the din.

I nodded. She reached around my hip and flipped up the depressed red button on my individual alarm. The pandemonium ceased.

"False alarm," she called out. The throng took a collective breath before retreating back behind their office doors.

"Happens to everyone," the woman said, and locked the main door. "Always check the red button when you get your keys. And," she added, bending down to scoop up said keys from the floor where I'd apparently flung them, "don't lose these. That would really be trouble."

"It won't happen again," I said. "Sorry."

"I'm Kate Henry, the Unit C manager," she said, and smiled. "Welcome to Napa State."

I stood for a moment in the empty hallway. From just outside the main door a distinct "ha-ha-ha" echoed up and down the concourse. It took a second to realize the sound was a peacock.

The door to Unit C was made of reinforced steel and had a small double-paned window. Inserting my key into the lock, I had just cracked the door open when a face appeared in the window.

The wild-eyed young man had hopelessly tangled hair and wore rumpled baby-blue scrubs. He gestured frantically. "This is 88.5 National Public Radio," he said in a spot-on announcer's voice. "Donate to our pledge drive. Don't listen for free, that's stealing. Now here's Ofeibea Quist-Arcton." He spun three times, stopped on a dime, and flashed the familiar "jazz hands" pose before walking away.

I regained my composure and stepped fully inside the crowded hallway. A wooden chair whizzed past my left ear and smashed into the steel door like a gunshot.

Eyes red and prison muscles bulging, a tattooed white man behind me jumped to his feet from a crouch and swatted me aside. The back of my head smacked into the wall. Lights blinked. Something wet trickled down my neck.

He snatched up the thrown chair and crashed it down onto the head of a charging older black man, who crumpled into a heap.

"Don't ever fuck with me, old man!" the giant hissed, slinging the chair at the inert body. "You owe. You pay." He backed away and walked down the corridor as a file of terrified patients pressed themselves against the walls.

He cut past the glass-enclosed nurses' station, where a clutch of five women scattered with a terrified yelp as the big man slapped a hamlike hand on the window. One nurse pushed her hip alarm and the pulsing shriek rang out again.

"Never question who's the boss here," the man thundered above the din, and turned to glare at me. He stood barefoot, his neck covered with interlocking black tattooed swirls, the word *HELL* inked into his forehead.

"The voices made me do it," he said, and theatrically clutched both sides of his head. Pivoting on his heels, he casually strolled out toward a nearby walled courtyard. "Don't forget to make a pledge," NPR-man said, and scuttled behind. "Safeway Corporation will match it."

CHAPTER TWO

By the eighteenth century the original "complete madness" definition for an insanity defense had evolved into the "wild beast" test. Under this test, the insanity defense was available to a person who was "totally depraved of his understanding so as to not know what he was doing, no more than an infant, a brute, or a wild beast."

–Herbert Feigl

Before becoming a psychiatrist, I'd been an ER doctor for eleven years. As the nurse clicked off the alarm, the old emergency physician in me kicked in. I dropped to my knees and cradled the downed man's gushing head between both legs to keep his neck stable.

Blood streaked my shirt and pants, it pooled and congealed on the floor. A thin trail of brain matter leaked from the man's crushed left temple.

Behind me the unit door opened and, responding to the alarm, a dozen staff members from Unit B upstairs and two cops ran in. The cops were directed to the courtyard while the extra staff started crowd control.

"Flashlight, please," I called, and a nurse pulled a small penlight from her shirt pocket and quickly passed it to me. I clicked on the beam, raised each of the fallen man's eyelids with a thumb, and shined the light into one eye, then the other. His right pupil constricted but the left barely moved and had begun to dilate. This was bad. It meant bleeding inside his head.

"We need the paramedics now!" I shouted.

"On the way," Kate Henry called back, the unit phone cradled on her shoulder.

With so much blood and pandemonium, the remaining patients stood quietly terrified. They'd scarcely moved when, five minutes later, the unit doors opened again. A three-person paramedic crew appeared with a gurney and carry board.

"Hit in the head with a chair," I said, and gently slid back. "He's got a blown pupil."

"I'm on it," one medic replied, and placed a stabilizing neck collar on the prone man. Beside me, a second medic ripped off the man's shirt and slapped round EKG leads onto his chest. To my right, a third man started an IV line.

"Alert County General ER," the first paramedic barked. "We'll need Life-Flight stat."

"County General on the line," Kate Henry called. A medic dashed over and spoke rapidly into the phone while the two other medics, three nurses, and I carefully placed the stricken patient on the carry board, then everyone lifted the load onto the gurney.

We helped secure the man with straps, then the crew hurried away. Cole, a new hospital cop I'd met during orientation, waved an arm and a tide of collateral staff flowed out behind the paramedic crew. With a final wham, the unit doors closed and locked.

Blood covered the floor. The patients stared. My head swam. I tried to stand but didn't think my knees would hold.

From the courtyard, the two cops calmly walked the huge tattooed man back to his room, closed the door, and stood watch outside.

"Medications!" shouted Nurse Luella Cortes, a midtwenties Hispanic woman. The patients, still stunned but apparently familiar with the drill, collected into a scraggly line before a small medication-room Dutch door.

I found a sink and threw water on my face. I scraped some blood off my neck and cleaned up as best I could. The rest of the staff had drifted back into the nurses' station.

Ben Cohen stood with the others—thirty-four, tall, handsome, sharp as a tack, our new unit psychologist. He'd been part of my orientation team as well. In all the hubbub, I'd missed him. This was his first day, too. He looked more heated than bewildered.

"That lunatic," Cohen fumed. "Who did he hit?"

"The injured man's name is Ralph Wilkins," said Mazie Monabong, a middle-aged Filipina nurse. "The man who hit him is Bill McCoy. They apparently had issues; probably a gambling debt."

"Or Wilkins didn't pay enough protection money," Palanqui said.

"Wilkins has been doing McCoy's laundry," Kate Henry added. "He owed him for something."

My temples started to throb. I turned to check the back of my head in a small mirror above the station sink. Kate Henry stepped over.

"Are you hurt?" she asked, and gently felt above my collar. Her fingertips came away with blood.

A wiry, middle-aged Asian man—"Xiang," read his name tag—pulled up a chair behind me.

"Sit, please," Xiang said. Slight but sturdy, Xiang wore an air of no-nonsense.

"I'll be okay. It's nothing really," I replied.

"Sit, please," Xiang repeated, and I did. He donned a pair of latex gloves from a box on the nearby counter and began to sort through my hair.

"This will need stitches," he said, and dabbed my head with a square of gauze.

"I don't think stitches are necessary," I countered, and tried to stand, but Xiang's hand gently pressed on my shoulder.

"You're the new doctor, right?" he asked, and eased me back down.

"Yes, I'm Doctor Seager," I replied.

Xiang daubed my cut with a fresh piece of cotton.

"Mr. Xiang is our head nurse," Kate Henry explained.

"Nice to—" I began, but Xiang cut me off.

"We haven't had a doctor on Unit C for months," he said, still heeding to my wound. "We need you. We need you really bad." He gently rotated the stool and looked me in the eye. "You don't get that cut fixed," he said, "then maybe you get an infection, then maybe you get tetanus, and maybe you die. Maybe we don't have a doctor here for three more months or a year or maybe ever." He paused and smiled. "Please, get the cut fixed."

My head was a pounding drum. "Okay," I said.

Xiang pulled three sheaves of paper from a tall stack on a nearby desk and hastily scrawled at the bottom of each.

"Take these to the ER at County General," he said. "Randy will drive you. He's our tech." A good-looking young black man stood, collected the papers from Xiang, and walked up beside me.

"Don't worry," Cohen said. "I'll find out everything we need to know about McCoy."

"Thanks" was all I could muster.

"Hope you feel better," Monabong called behind us as Randy and I headed out.

Near the station doorway, we passed a trio of staff members, trailed by a fourth nurse with a poised, fully loaded syringe. They corralled the two cops standing guard and disappeared into McCoy's room.

WE WALKED THROUGH the County General ER door, and the sign-in clerk recognized my name tag. She took Xiang's papers from Randy and called a nurse who, despite a loaded waiting room, escorted us right back into a curtained cubicle.

"I'll be fine," I said to Randy. "You can go back."

Randy hesitated, nodded, then left.

As I waited, above the general din of a busy ER I heard, from the pod behind mine, frenetic footsteps and strained, sharp voices, the shred of plastic, the clang of a mobile X-ray machine, the rattle of IV poles: the clamor of a battle with death.

"I'm Dr. Vezo," a young woman in a white coat said as she parted the cubicle curtain and walked in. "Let's take a peek at that." She set down a clipboard, stepped behind me, and parsed the hair on the back of my head. "How'd this happen?" she asked.

"I hit my head," I replied as Vezo pulled on sterile gloves, anesthetized and washed my cut with Betadine, and then began to suture.

"Are you from Napa, too?" Vezo said when she'd finished.

"I am from Napa," I said, then sat up and turned to face her. "Do you get a lot of this stuff from there?"

"Stuff . . . ?"

"How much violence goes on there?"

"We see a fair bit," Vezo replied, and peeled off her gloves. "You know what they call Napa State around here?"

I shook my head.

"Gomorrah," Vezo said. "As in 'Sodom and . . .' It's a mysterious place. Nobody really knows what kind of bad shit goes on inside there."

My head started to hurt and for a moment I thought I might have made a very bad job decision. But I didn't say that. "I think things will be okay," I said.

Before Vezo could speak again, she was paged to the trauma room stat. "We have extra scrubs in back," she said quickly, and gestured to my bloodstained clothes, then snagged her clipboard, opened the curtain, and was gone.

I pulled out my cell phone, uncertain what to say to my wife.

"Hi, Ingrid. I'm at County General ER," I said.

"Are you all right?" Ingrid asked, alarmed.

"I bumped my head. Nothing to worry about. But I do need a ride."

"I'll be there as soon as I can," she said.

I wandered to the back of the ER, changed into a set of green County General scrubs, put my soiled clothes into a plastic sack, and walked outside amid the roar of a nearby helicopter landing.

I spotted a bench beneath a shady tree and sat down. The air was cool and still.

When Ingrid arrived I smiled. Tall, blond, elegant inside and out, she emerged from her silver SUV and walked up to me.

"It's just a cut," I said, and touched the back of my head.

Ingrid reached around and parted my hair. "You have ten stitches," she said, clearly upset. "Who did this to you?" A physician as well, she'd seen her share of blood. But family's always different.

"We need to get my truck," I said, and stepped toward the SUV. "I'll tell you everything on the way."

"I found this in the driveway," Ingrid said, and handed me a copy of the hospital map Dr. Francis had sent me. It had somehow fallen out of my pocket. "Napa State Hospital" was printed across the top of the paper.

"Napa State," I said. "In the ER just now they called it Gomorrah."

"What?" Ingrid asked.

"Gomorrah, like 'Sodom and . . .'" I said. "Who knows what really goes on inside there . . . ?"

"What . . . ?"

I looked at the map again. Inside the fence, Unit C had been circled. "I'm sorry," I said. "I should have told you."

Ingrid started the car and eased out of the County General lot.

"At the last minute I got reassigned to Unit C," I said. "They said we wouldn't be going inside the fence, but apparently something changed. I wanted to check out the place first. I thought you might worry."

Ingrid pulled up to a light.

"I walked onto my new unit," I continued, "and a guy the size of a mountain with the word *HELL* tattooed across his forehead smacked me into a wall, then beat an old man senseless with a chair. He fractured the man's skull. They just flew him out."

Ingrid is Danish with a natural Scandinavian reserve, not one to show feelings. "You should have told me about the unit change," she sighed. "But that doesn't matter now. I don't know what to say. I'm frightened. It's your first day of work, and you get your head smashed. You were only there an hour."

"On the bright side," I said, attempting a smile, "things probably won't get much worse."

I must have hit my head harder than I thought, because after that, I don't remember much about the afternoon. When John, our fourteen-year-old son, arrived home, I was on the couch, staring blankly at *Days of Our Lives.*

"You're home?" John asked, and glanced quizzically at the TV. "Watching soaps?" Then he stopped. "Is your head bleeding, Dad? What happened?"

Some blood had trickled down my neck. I don't recall what transpired after that.

By evening, my thoughts had cleared and I felt better. Ingrid reexamined my cut and gently stanched any fresh weeping.

Over dinner, attempting damage control, I rehashed a sanitized version of the day's story for John. Wise beyond his years, he shook his head. "Dad, you can't work there," he said. "It's not safe."

Later that night, I sat on the edge of the bed as Ingrid removed her makeup and washed her face.

As she did, I retold the story of the sally port and described the campus. I told her about the false alarm, which brought a weary smile.

I stood and stared out a window that overlooked the distant lights of town. "I've never been so scared," I said.

Ingrid toweled off her cheeks and turned toward me. "Isn't Napa or Gomorrah or whatever they call it supposed to be a hospital?" she asked, her tone measured.

I didn't have an answer.

"And if it's like you say, John's right, you can't go back. There are other jobs. I can't see you hurt. Nothing's worth that."

"Let me think about it," I said.

I didn't know much about state forensic hospitals when I applied at Gomorrah—as most people, even psychiatrists, don't either. I knew state facilities cared for the sickest of the sick, the real-life Hannibal Lecters of the world. I'd sent patients to Metropolitan State Hospital, one of five forensic hospitals in California, when I'd worked in Los Angeles. But I'd never been inside one. Nor did I know anyone who had. I'd never really thought much about them. They aren't discussed much in psychiatric circles. They're just there. Out in the countryside somewhere. And no one knows what violent, dangerous places they really are.

Drifting off to sleep, I remembered the sack of bloody clothes with my favorite blue tie stuffed in the pants pocket. I never saw that bag again.

CHAPTER THREE

I'm nobody
I'm a tramp, a bum, a hobo
I'm a boxcar and a jug of wine
And a straight razor . . .
If you get too close to me

—**Charles Manson**

A few months back, I'd stumbled across the ad for the Napa State job and read the details aloud to Ingrid. We were at a serious financial crossroads, and both knew we needed to make a change.

I'd married Ingrid in 1998 while she was in residency training and still had a pile of student loans. A year later, John was born. Then, in 2007, we bought our first house and, like so many others, we were snared by the Great Recession of 2008.

Our jobs were suddenly unsteady. Ingrid's hospital announced big changes. Employers gutted our pension plans. Incomes shriveled. We thought we might lose our home.

Luckily, Ingrid applied for and landed a job at a large hospital in Northern California. That got us halfway home. I scoured classified ads in medical journals and, after a series of misfires, came upon an advertisement for Napa State Hospital.

Journal in hand, I walked over to where Ingrid sat. She put down her book. "It's only thirty miles from your new hospital," I said.

Ingrid took the periodical and perused the section I'd circled. "Have you heard of this place?" she asked.

"It's a state mental hospital. They treat the sickest patients," I said.

"You're good with really sick people," Ingrid said.

"It seems like what we've been looking for," I added.

Ingrid brightened. "It sounds terrific." She handed me back the periodical. "I say go for it."

"I've already asked for an application."

I filled out the application, personally interviewed twice, and then waited anxiously. Ingrid, John, our furniture, and our two dogs, Mulder and Scully—a black Border Collie and a Jack Russell terrier—went on ahead. Ingrid found a rental home and they settled in. While Ingrid began her new job, I ate 7-Eleven hot dogs and take-out Chinese food, slept on the floor, and spoke with real estate agents about the sale of our home. In the process, I learned depressing new terms like *underwater* and *short sale*.

One day an email arrived. "Congratulations," it began. I'd been hired at Napa State. I gave my current job notice, tied up loose ends, and in record time jammed my personal belongings into the back of my truck and rejoined my family.

Ingrid and I knew how lucky we were. At the last minute, we'd both been thrown life preservers. Our heads were barely above water, but for the first time in a couple of years, we could actually see the surface.

Now, I heard Ingrid's alarm beeping and I headed to the kitchen. Suddenly needing some air, I stepped out through the sliding glass door, bent over, and puked into the bushes beside the deck. The dogs barked.

"Jesus Christ," I said, and wiped my mouth. "What are you, a scared ten-year-old?"

Heart pounding, my head about to split, I made a decision.

In thirty minutes, everyone had eaten and dressed. Ingrid and I were in the entryway. John had gone to get his schoolbooks.

"You're going to work, then?" Ingrid asked.

"Yes."

"Are you sure about this?"

"No," I said. "But if I don't go back, I could never explain to John what it means to face your fears."

"John just wants you to be safe," Ingrid said.

"I think it will be a good lesson for him," I added.

"Don't put this on John," Ingrid said. "Just please be careful."

DAY TWO. I approached the metal door to Unit C, took a breath, and looked through the small window. The hallway seemed quiet. I opened the door and walked inside.

Halfway to the nurses' station, McCoy emerged from a doorway and stepped directly in front of me. King Kong and I stood chest to face. He blotted out the hallway lights.

"You the new doctor?" McCoy said, and casually leered down.

"I-I'm Dr. Seager," I stuttered, my mouth dry.

The colossus broke out into a big, gap-toothed smile. "Welcome to Unit C," he said. "I'm Bill McCoy. Nice to meet you." He held out a jumbo-sized hand, which I shook weakly. "Sorry about yesterday, Doc," McCoy added. "You okay? Someone said you bumped your head."

"It was nothing," I blurted, and tapped my stitches.

"Well, anyway, sorry for the fuss," McCoy said. "Some personal business needed tending. You're a doctor, you know better than me: can't let a cancer fester."

"I understand."

McCoy lumbered back toward his room. "You need anything, Doc, see me, hear?" he said over his shoulder.

"Sure."

Thankfully, a rare lull lay over the nurses' station. Everyone looked up when I walked in. "Welcome back, Doc," Xiang said.

"How's the head?" Kate Henry asked.

"It's fine," I assured her. "At least on the outside."

"Great to see you again," Cohen said, and entered the station door behind me. "I've got the dirt on McCoy. I went through his chart yesterday while you were gone. Very interesting."

I turned to see a slew of patients walking by the window, headed to the adjacent walled courtyard for their scheduled fresh-air break. McCoy appeared and passed in review, waving lazily to us minions on the way out.

"Shouldn't he be in jail or something?" I said. "He nearly killed a man."

Xiang hoisted a thick black binder off the station desk and headed toward the door.

"Everybody here killed someone," he said, and disappeared into the hallway. The bulk of the staff followed.

Palanqui nudged me from behind. "You don't want to be left in here alone, do you?" She smiled.

We walked a short distance down the hallway, Xiang unlocked a door, and everyone entered a conference room—although "conference room" may have been a bit generous. It was a small, windowless cubicle filled with a table and ten wooden chairs of the type McCoy had used to truncheon Wilkins in the hallway. We took our seats, Xiang set down the binder, and morning rounds began.

At the start of each hospital day, all unit patients are discussed in varying degrees of detail and their care plan for the day is determined. As a former assistant professor at UCLA medical school, I'd done such rounds thousands of times.

"We had a problem last night," Xiang announced, hands folded atop the black binder. "Night shift smelled cigarette smoke in the hallway," he said. "They checked Mr. Leon Smith's room and found him running a craps game. The usual: smoke in the air, patients in a circle, coins on the floor. Caught Mr. Smith with dice in his hand."

"Wasn't Wilkins Mr. Smith's roommate?" Palanqui asked.

"They moved Wilkins's bed aside," Xiang said. "Made more room for the game."

"For some patients, empathy isn't a strength," Monabong said.

"Let me guess," Luella Cortes added with mock alarm. "Mr. Chen and Mr. Richmond were in attendance?"

"Correct," Kate Henry sighed.

Luella turned to me. "Unit C is easy to understand," she said, and pointed toward the door. "You want gambling: North Wing. Drugs: South Wing. Prostitution: East. And"—she shook her head and lowered her arm—"the West Wing belongs to Mr. McCoy. There you can get anything."

"It's really thoughtful the way the patients have divided things up," Charlene Larsen chimed in. She was a lanky black social worker in her fifties. "It's like a little navigation system."

"Prostitution?" I backtracked, but no one answered. I thought I might have heard wrong.

"Can the team please speak to Mr. Smith today?" Xiang continued.

"Of course," I stated, and the others concurred.

Xiang opened the black binder, and for the next hour the group discussed the diagnoses, medications, and general treatment blueprint for all forty Unit C residents. I added comments where appropriate, as did the others.

"We have Walk Group at nine," Larsen said. "I'll need someone to go with me."

"I'll help," Palanqui said. "But I need to be back for Symptom Management at eleven."

"Four guys are going to school," Kate Henry said. "They'll get picked up at ten, usual time."

"School?" I said.

"We have a full curriculum," Kate Henry said. "And certified teachers. We offer a high school diploma program and can arrange for college work."

After seeing McCoy and the other patients on Unit C, I tried to imagine that classroom.

"Legal Issues meets at one," Cohen continued. "And Unit Government at three."

"I have Art Group at two," the unit's recreational therapist said.

"Don't forget Phone Group," Randy interjected. "And tonight is movie night. *Star Wars: Episode Three.*"

"Are things always this busy?" I asked.

"Idle hands, Devil's workshop," Xiang said.

"Where do you run these groups?"

"Most are here on the unit, or in the building," Palanqui said.

"Does anyone sit in with you?" I asked. "Hospital police, maybe?"

"Of course not," Kate Henry said. "Therapy can't happen with a cop at your elbow."

Before I could reply, we switched gears. Xiang opened the black binder to a new section.

"Dr. Seager, you and Dr. Cohen are new," he said. "We go through each person's crimes once. Important to know these things."

Xiang turned a page. He spoke in the uninflected monotone voice one uses when handling familiar material. In alphabetical order, he named each patient and followed with a terse explanation of their crimes. Most had committed murder, some multiple times. Others were rapists of both women and children, also often repeat offenders. A few men fit both categories; they'd raped their victims, then killed them. Almost universally, drugs or alcohol had been involved.

"There's actually a definition of *mass murder*," Cohen said when Xiang paused. "I looked it up. You have to kill at least four people at one time in a single location. That's different from a spree killer, who kills his victims one after the other during a single time span but in different locations.

"Serial killers, on the other hand," Cohen continued, "only have to kill three people. But they do it at different times and in various geographic areas. Ted Bundy, that kind of thing. Men usually kill for revenge, to right some perceived wrong done to them. They kill their boss, coworkers, parents, or strangers. Women tend to kill their kids."

Monabong looked askance at Cohen. "You read about things like that?" she said.

Undaunted, Xiang pressed on. "Cervantes, Miguel," he said. "He wears the paper Zorro mask with pink washcloths in his ears."

I'd seen the man walk by but had forgotten to ask about him.

"What's up with that guy?" Cohen asked.

"Washcloths are an improvement over what he did before," Palanqui added, and the Unit C old-timers grimaced.

"Used to smear feces all over his face," Xiang said. "We cleaned him two or three times every day. Got stuck in his nose. Big mess."

I felt a twinge of nausea.

"Mr. Cervantes has been ill since age ten," Xiang went on. "A few years ago he stopped his psych meds, wandered away from his board-and-care home, the family lost contact. A year later he raped two girls, ages six and seven. Strangled them and buried their bodies in the park."

"After a week," Randy said, "a guy was walking his dog and the dog dug them up."

I said nothing and Xiang continued, "Hong, his roommate, similar story. Been sick a long time. Stopped his medications. Killed his mother. She came home from work. Mr. Hong stood in the doorway and shot her with an assault rifle. He reloaded four times. Then he used a saw and cut her into pieces, boxed them up, and tried to mail the boxes."

"Police detained him," Luella added, "while he was cramming the bloody packages into a corner mailbox."

"Mr. Hong thought his mom was having sex with Satan," Randy said.

Xiang read more names and detailed more crimes. Then he paused. "Tomlin, Michael," he said. "Blew up an elementary school."

"Fortunately it was after regular hours," Kate Henry added. "But he still killed six kids and a teacher."

"I remember hearing about that," I said, startled. "About five years back? If I recall, he'd molested some girls from that same school?"

"Mr. Tomlin has been sick a long time, too," Xiang continued. "He also stopped his medications. Did crack cocaine instead. After one year, he blew up the school."

"Which one's Tomlin?" I asked.

"He's the man who talks about NPR all the time," Luella said.

Xiang went on. He spoke of Mr. Harlan West, who stabbed a stranger with a box cutter, then flayed off his skin. Mr. Oliver Burns, killed his wife, cut her up, and cooked her. "Landlady complained of the smell," Xiang said. "He killed her, too." And Mr. Villegas, who buried his father alive in the backyard.

Xiang mentioned others, but after a while everything just blurred into one big conglomeration of grim murder, violent rape, dismemberment, and abuse.

"I get the idea," I said as we passed the halfway point. I looked at my watch and pretended time was an issue. "Perhaps I can read the rest later?"

Mercifully, Xiang closed the binder.

Despite my discomfort, I needed to know one more thing.

"What about McCoy?" I said.

Cohen perked up. "McCoy killed a gas station attendant," he stated. "Police report says they tangled over a pack of chewing gum. He demolished the cashier's glass cage, dragged the man through the ragged shards, then decapitated him with a chunk of broken window.

"But here's the interesting part," Cohen continued. "Turns out he's killed two other people as well. Beat one to death with a cinder block. Hacked up the other with a garden hoe. Got off both times. He said voices told him to do it. He did a six-year stint at Atascadero State Hospital, down the road near San Luis Obispo, then a stretch at Patton State Hospital outside LA. All the cases look like stipulated decisions. PC 1370 ICST for one and PC 1026 NGRI for the other. But the stories are all the same: he was high on meth every time."

"What do the letters and numbers stand for?" I asked.

"PC means 'penal code,'" Cohen said. "The numbers 1370 and 1026 indicate the section in the state law code that applies to each case. The other stuff, the acronyms, are forensic shorthand for at what exact point in the crime process you were nuts. So NGRI, not guilty by reason of insanity, means you were bonkers when you did the crime. ICST, incompetent to stand trial, says you may have been fine when you killed the guy, but you're nuts when you go to trial. Basically the letters and numbers tell you the legal and psychiatric reasons the person skated and ended up here."

Cohen and I had gotten to know each other pretty well during our week of orientation. He was new to Unit C, like me, but apparently had been working ahead.

I mentally blocked out the next few evenings for some serious reading. "And stipulated decisions?"

"That's when the district attorney and public defender both agree that a person's too loony to prosecute and not responsible for his crime," Cohen said. "The judge goes along and sends them here."

"Sounds a little iffy," I said.

"It's a Friday-afternoon thing," Cohen concluded. "Everybody's tired. Who wants a big argument?"

CHAPTER FOUR

I should never have been convicted of anything more serious than running a cemetery without a license. They were just a bunch of worthless little queers and punks.

—John Wayne Gacy, after twenty-eight bodies were dug up under his house. Gacy, known as the "Killer Clown," strangled thirty-three teenage boys and young men. He performed as a clown at children's parties.

"During that mess yesterday," I said as rounds wound down, "did someone mention McCoy and protection money?"

"Either you pay him," Monabong said, "or he beats the crap out of you."

"Or he demands your family send money to his family," Palanqui added. "He casts a wide net."

"And not just patients and family," Xiang said. "He threatened staff, too. Don't get mixed up with McCoy. Mr. Wilkins learned this the hard way."

"And the hospital police know about all this, right?" I said.

"Of course," Xiang stated. "They say Mr. McCoy is under investigation."

"That doesn't sound too promising," I said.

"Sounds like bullshit to me," Cohen huffed.

"Does McCoy need more medication?" I asked.

"McCoy doesn't take medication," Palanqui said.

"Mr. McCoy isn't mentally ill," Luella said. "He's a meth head."

"Somehow," Cohen added, "he keeps convincing some lame judge that he's crazy."

"That man is crazy like a fox," Monabong said.

My anxiety mounted. "Is everyone here a criminal?" I asked.

I knew state mental hospitals took care of psychopaths: James Holmes, Andrea Yates, Son of Sam—that kind of thing. I just didn't realize there'd be so many of them.

"Almost everyone here comes from court," Xiang said. "They send us violent criminals who are also mentally ill. Or who pretend to be mentally ill."

"We get sick, violent criminals instead of the state prisons?" I asked.

"We pride ourselves on that fact," Kate Henry said.

"But prisons have guns and guards," I replied. "We have art therapy and a bunch of nurses."

"All our staff are expertly trained in conflict management," Kate Henry said, and an uncomfortable pall fell around the table.

"Of course," Cohen said.

Kate Henry's eyes flashed. "Our work here speaks for itself." Another pause.

"You mentioned 'almost' everyone comes from court," I said.

"Ninety percent."

"And the other ten percent?"

"Just mentally ill," Xiang replied. "Mainly all the older guys now. They came before we started taking convicts and never left. Some lived here all their lives."

"I remember," Larsen said sadly, "when that's all we had. Back before the courts took over the system and threw our patients into the street."

"Is the court still involved here?" I asked.

Cohen jumped in, "I was told we write a letter every six months on each patient, explaining to the judge how the person is doing, why he's still sick, and why he's still dangerous."

I'd written a number of court letters over the years. "I'm guessing that if the patient or his attorney disagrees with our assessment," I said, "then we go to court to defend our conclusions and testify against our patients."

"I believe so," Cohen replied.

"Who protects the mentally ill guys like Wilkins from the convicts?" I asked.

"We do," Kate Henry responded.

"Who protects us?"

"We always have these," Cohen said, and tapped the individual alarm on his hip. "Maybe you can whip it off and throw it at someone."

Kate Henry remained impassive.

"If these guys are all prisoners," I said, "why don't we have guards?"

"Hospitals don't have guards," Kate Henry said curtly.

"But—" I started when Xiang cut me off.

"We're moving on now," he said. "Unit business for this morning. Mr. Roger West, dental appointment at eleven."

"Didn't Villegas knock out West's front teeth?" Palanqui asked.

"West's dental appointment was canceled," Randy interjected. "I saw the sheet on the fax machine. Dental only performs extractions. And that's already been done."

"Villegas has a date with wound clinic this afternoon," Luella said. "He's got some ugly cuts on his knuckles. Looks like MRSA."

After a few more bullet points, Xiang closed the black book, but no one stood.

"Does anyone have a casualty report?" Monabong sighed.

"News on Mr. Wilkins?" Xiang began, and glanced at me.

"He was flown out from County General yesterday," I said. "I saw the helicopter leave."

"Mr. Wilkins is a nice man," Palanqui added. "He likes Art Group. He's an excellent painter."

"You nearly murder someone, don't you go to jail?" I said, baffled. "Why is McCoy still here?"

"Maybe the police will come and arrest him," Xiang said. "And take him to jail. But jail always sends these people right back. We know how that goes."

"How what goes?" I asked.

Luella touched my arm. "McCoy's already in the state nuthouse, probably for life," she said. "The prisons don't want these guys. That's why they send them here to begin with. Mental illness scares them."

"So McCoy assaults anyone he likes?" I persisted.

"What can we do?" Xiang said.

I sat, stunned into silence.

"Any news about Dr. Tom?" Palanqui asked. She looked pinched—like merely forming the words of her question had been painful.

"Wife says he's become nonresponsive," Xiang stated in obvious but well-modulated distress. "The last CT scan showed more blood in his brain. The family isn't hopeful."

"He's been in and out of the ICU for months," Monabong added. "And it's always the same report: more bleeding. Can't they do something?"

I collected my nerve. "Who is Dr. Tom?" I asked. "What happened?"

Xiang sat forward. "Dr. Tom was our unit psychiatrist. And a good one. You took his place. One day, Mr. Alex Mathews in room eleven found a piece of broken metal sprinkler pipe in the exercise yard. Somehow he sneaked it onto the unit," Xiang said slowly. "I don't know how, we search everything so carefully.

"After lunch, Mr. Mathews stood behind the door to his room," Xiang continued. "Mr. Vernon Chambers, his roommate, asked the staff if he could speak to a doctor. So Dr. Tom walked in." Xiang's left leg bounced ever so finely. "Mr. Mathews hit Dr. Tom on the head with the pipe, knocked him out, kicked him over and over. Dr. Tom has been in a coma since then; his skull was broken. He bled into his brain."

"Mr. Mathews was angry," Palanqui said, "because Dr. Tom had stopped Mr. Mathews's regular OxyContin pill a week before. The night nurses caught him hiding the pills in his cheeks and then selling them to the other patients."

"Mr. Mathews broke his own wrist," Luella added. "That's how he got the OxyContin in the first place."

"They've operated on Dr. Tom three times," Larsen said despondently. "But nothing seems to work."

"He's forty-two," Kate Henry said. "He and his wife, Ellen, have two kids, seven and five, and another on the way."

I had to remember to breathe.

"Surely Mr. Mathews went to jail?" I mumbled.

"For a month. But he's back in room eleven," Xiang said. "Go to jail, doesn't matter. Stay awhile, but these people act crazy. They all come back."

The threads of conversation slowly frayed, then dropped. The silence was broken when Cohen motioned to my head. "How's the cut?" he asked.

"Fine," I replied. "It wasn't much."

"Sorry I couldn't help."

"Thanks. But there wasn't anything you could have done."

"You never know," Cohen countered. "I'm big for a psychologist."

"I'm sure that's why you were sent here."

"This shit is going to stop," Cohen said, a fist clenched.

We made our way into the hallway and walked back toward the nurses' station. Lost in thought, I felt a tug on my sleeve.

"Doc," a man whispered conspiratorially. "I have to get out of here." I saw a mass of tangled dark hair. "You have to let me go now," the voice continued. "It's not safe."

He turned his face up. I was confronted with the paper Zorro mask and bright pink washcloths jammed into both ears. The man looked like a neon puppy crossed with a raccoon.

"Mr. Cervantes," I said. "What do you need?"

"I warned Dr. Tom but he didn't listen," Cervantes said. "Now I'm warning you." He nodded toward the other patients in the hall and whispered, "I'm not nuts and they're not nuts. This *place* is nuts. Get me out now or you'll die in here with us." His pink ears wagged as he spoke.

CHAPTER FIVE

What word do you think of most?

1. Kill/Burn

2. Monkeys

3. Hmm . . . . . .

4. I don't know!

—Quiztron, "Are you criminally insane?"

Taken aback by the hair, paper mask, and pink ears, I hadn't noticed at first that Cervantes spoke to me in the crowded hallway while stark naked.

"You're naked," I said finally, and looked around for help.

"And you're stupid," Cervantes replied.

"You've got washcloths in your ears," I countered, stalling for time. Xiang and Luella trotted toward us, blankets in hand.

"I don't make idle threats," Cervantes spat, and opened his right hand to reveal a thin metal rod with a sharp point. "Get me out of here or I'll drive this through your fucking head."

Just then Xiang and Luella arrived. They quickly wrapped Cervantes in two blankets and shuttled him toward his room at the end of the hallway.

"He's got a piece of sharp—" I said.

"Dr. Seager," a tall, linebacker-large black man shouted, and hurried toward me. Squarely in the path of a blue freight train, I reached for my alarm button but pawed the wrong hip. I snatched a breath as the locomotive screeched to a stop.

"Don't you remember?" the man blurted. "Tom Caruthers?"

I was so relieved I nearly peed my pants. I'd heard his name at rounds but hadn't made the connection.

"Mr. Caruthers, what are you doing here?" I sputtered. I'd been his doctor twenty years before, during the four years of my psychiatry residency training. A troubled youth with a terrible sickness, Caruthers had been in and out of the LA County mental hospital a dozen times. We'd spoken often and at great length.

Our relationship had always been complicated. Alcohol, drugs, and violence riddled the family. During his teenage years, I was the only functional adult in Caruthers's life.

Unexpectedly seeing Caruthers again put everything back into focus. "I heard you got into some serious trouble?"

"If you've got time, I'll tell you," Caruthers replied.

"We'll speak this afternoon," I said as behind me Xiang headed toward the nurses' station. "I promise."

"Excellent," Caruthers enthused. "See you then." He turned and walked away.

I hurried after Xiang.

"Mr. Cervantes had a piece of sharp metal in his hand," I said, opening the station door. "He threatened to stab me with it."

"He made a serious threat?" Xiang said.

"He sounded serious," I said.

"You saw the sharp metal?" Xiang asked.

"Yes."

"Shank!" Xiang shouted. He leaned over next to the station phone and grabbed a large microphone.

"Lockdown, gentlemen, lockdown," Xiang boomed into the mike. His words echoed up and down the tiled hallways.

Xiang turned his head. "Hospital police, now," he ordered Luella, who snatched up the desk phone and punched zero.

"Lockdown on Unit C," Luella said crisply. "We've got a shank."

"Lockdown, gentlemen, lockdown," Xiang said into the mike again, then looked at me. "Loud noise." He flipped a switch on the wall next to the station door.

I flattened both hands over my ears as a hellish air-raid siren began to wail and strobe lights flashed.

Xiang grabbed my arm and motioned to Cohen, who stood near us, and we ran down to Cervantes's room.

"We need to get him before he hides it," Xiang shouted, and threw open Cervantes's door. Cervantes stood in the middle of the room, now dressed in scrubs.

"Open your hands," Xiang shouted, and Cervantes did. No metal. Xiang patted Cervantes from head to toe and wrinkled every seam in his shirt and pants. "Nothing," he said.

Cohen and I scurried around the room. We came up empty as well.

"I saw a piece of sharp metal," I said, straining above the din.

"He hid it somewhere," Xiang barked. "We don't find it, we get an X-ray." Then we headed out.

In the hallway, performing a well-rehearsed dance, staff members guided patients to their rooms. Tiny women steered the arms of men twice their size. Occasional shouts of protest rang out, but the blinding lights kept resistance to a minimum.

With each patient sealed in his room and the unit doors locked, Xiang pulled a set of keys from his pocket, stuck one into a wall panel, and turned. Mercifully, the flash and wail stopped.

My ears rang, but I could still discern the distant whine of police cars.

"Don't miss *Car Talk*," NPR-man said under his door. "Tom and Ray, the zany *Car Talk* brothers, will answer your automotive questions."

The lockdown produced a muscular police response. Twelve officers, Cole among them, arrived, accompanied by two large brindle-and-tan German shepherds, each in a padded harness attached to a short rope. Bangban, the young cop I'd encountered yesterday in the sally port, held both leashes tightly.

The officers wore Kevlar jackets, carried batons, and had high-tech helmets on their heads, last names stenciled on the brow. They gathered around Xiang.

"Dr. Seager saw a shank," Xiang said.

The men looked at me, as did the dogs.

"Mr. Cervantes had a piece of sharp metal in his hand," I stated.

"Where is it now?" Bangban asked.

"We searched him and the room," Xiang said. "Found nothing."

"X-ray?" Bangban asked.

"Not yet," Xiang said.

Lieutenant Harrison—a gold star on his silver helmet, tall, wide shoulders, military bearing—yanked a spiral-bound notebook from his back pocket and opened the cover. "Did it look like anything in here?" he said, and passed me the folder, which contained four dozen snapshots of homemade weapons lying at odd angles, with a standard wooden ruler beside each. They all looked coarse but effective. I pointed to a thin rod.

"That's it," I said.

"Eyeglass stem," Harrison shouted, then snatched the book from my hands and jammed it back into his hip pocket. "Let's go," he snapped.

In unison the officers paired up. Bangban re-gripped the dogs as the constables divided the four hallways between them. I watched the display, then noticed that Xiang and the rest of the staff had fallen in as well.

"Come on," Cohen said, and shrugged his shoulders. "This might be fun."

What followed was a shakedown, a maneuver in which the unit is meticulously searched for contraband.

The cops forced doors open, pushed patients up against walls, and swiftly frisked them. We helped turn up dresser drawers, flip mattresses, and search the crevices around each room's baseboards, door hinges, and light fixtures. I began to sort through loose articles of clothing, shake out books, and scour for small holes in the thick, frosted bathroom window glass, through which items may have been passed from the outside.

The dogs were also hard at work, sniffing each bed, closet, and even, despite their protests, the patients themselves.

Twice both hounds burst into a spasm of yelps and dug frantically. From a bureau drawer an officer pulled an envelope containing pills. In a laundry bag another cop found a small flask. He undid the cap and took a quick smell. "Alcohol," he said.

"Good dogs," Cole said, and petted each canine in turn.

Throughout the search, boots clambered and scraped across

linoleum floors, baton sticks thwacked bedding, and a cascade of debris from two dozen upended nightstands jangled onto the tile.

Initially, the patients pled innocence and disbelief, but that quickly evolved into righteous anger and indignation. Scuffles erupted. Inside room eleven, Cole took down a burly young black man, grappling him into submission. A small table got smashed. A dog howled. I noticed Larsen staring.

The fracas grew heated. The door slammed. I heard punches. Staff rushed in.

"Five points!" Xiang shouted, and a nurse scurried toward the restraint room.

I caught Xiang's eye. "Mr. Mathews," he said.

Restraints are applied to a dangerous person when physical harm to himself, another patient, or a staff member seems imminent. Trained staff shackle both wrists and ankles to the four corners of a bed in a spread-eagle position, called "four-point restraints." If containment isn't achieved, a fifth "point" is added: a belt around the thighs, waist, or chest to keep the patient from "bucking." And if spitting occurs, a spit mask, a mesh facial cover resembling a beekeeper's hat, is applied as well. Emergency medication is then administered by injection.

The restraint room contains a single bed behind a locked door. The agitated person is left alone but is closely observed until the situation comes under control. This process is known as "seclusion and restraint."

Cole left the room and the staff bustled Mathews away. Monabong opened the restraint room door and Mathews was wrestled inside.

"We need a med order," Xiang said from the medication room doorway.

"What do you usually use?" I asked.

"B52," Xiang answered.

"Good by me," I replied, and Xiang quickly drew up the concoction.

B52 is psychiatric shorthand for five milligrams of Haldol, a strong antipsychotic medication, mixed in a syringe with two milligrams of Ativan, a potent Valium-like drug, and two milligrams of Cogentin, a sedative. The cocktail can drop a horse.

With the dogs in the lead, our group turned to enter the next room. Cohen appeared at my side.

Along a near wall, I saw Caruthers and his roommate, Manuel Ortega, a frail, elderly Hispanic man in a wheelchair. Caruthers held my gaze until the cops summarily spun both patients around and executed a thorough search.

"Is that how you'd treat your father?" Caruthers spat when he thought the cops had mishandled his friend. The cops didn't blink or stop. After both men proved clean, the police turned their attention to the room.

While officers did the heavy lifting, I sifted through a few articles that lay randomly dumped on a bedspread and held up a Sharpie writing pen.

"Good work, Doc," Bangban said, and patted my arm. "Sharpie pen," he called out. "New doctor found it." Bangban ceremoniously dropped the pen into a plastic bag held by his partner.

"Better in a bag than someone's back," Xiang said.

As we turned to leave, Caruthers fixed his stare on me again. My neck felt hot. The cops walked out and, unnerved, I followed.

Our shakedown team continued to Cervantes's room. One by one we stacked up in the doorway, the eager dogs by our side. Cervantes, Zorro mask and washrags intact, stood by his roommate, Mr. Hong, a gracefully poised young Asian man with long blond pigtails and candy-apple-red nails. The pair clasped arms as we entered. The metal shank lay like a sacred offering in the center of a blanket on one of the two single beds in the room.

Bangban set down his baton, produced a pair of latex surgical gloves from a pants pocket, and stretched them on. He approached the thin pike on the bed as if it were radioactive. Cradling the instrument between a thumb and index finger, he gingerly held it to the light, then dropped it into his cohort's plastic sack.

I moved in closer. It was an eyeglass stem. The curved earpiece had been straightened and sharpened. It could easily have punched a hole in someone.

The crew searched the room while the cops frisked Cervantes and Hong, legs apart, palms on the wall. Then the dogs sniffed them both. Afraid of the animals, Hong recoiled and nearly fainted. Cervantes put an arm around his waist.

Their routine complete, the dogs stood down.

"Clean," Cole boomed.

"Mr. Cervantes, Mr. Hong, move now, please," Xiang insisted, and shepherded the two out the door. I watched Cervantes leave. His pink ear flags swayed as he rammed a closed fist into his left temple.

The team searched the room but turned up nothing else.

"Why did Cervantes give up the shank?" I asked as the team prepared to head out.

"Eyeglasses are easy to get," Xiang said. "Patient Rights says we can't restrict them. He made one, he'll make another."

"The shank he gave us," a nurse said, "might not even be the one you saw."

I took a last look around. "Where does he hide them?" I said, but everyone had already moved on.

The final room belonged to Bill McCoy. Cops from other groups joined the pack. On attack alert, the dogs stood poised.

McCoy had one of three single rooms on the unit. Dressed in fresh scrubs, he stood at the back of the room, relaxed against the window frame. As a garrison of grim-faced cops, billy clubs in hand, edged forward, McCoy squared and replied in kind. He stood stolid and unafraid. His tattooed arms hung like huge hams. A dog growled.

Then McCoy raised an arm. "Gentlemen," he said, "come in. I've been expecting you. Please forgive the mess. I don't entertain often and there was such short notice."

The cops seemed too stunned to move. But not Cohen. As if born to the task, he resolutely strode over to McCoy's bed, peeled off the covers, patted the mattress, ran a hand along a bookshelf, then dropped to his hands and knees and peered underneath the bed.

His face lit and he extracted a small mechanical contraption.

"You'd better wash your hands," McCoy said. "God knows where that's been."

"Tattoo machine," a tall cop interjected.

"Tattoo machine?" McCoy said with feigned hurt. "It's an ink-and-metal sculpture. I made it in Art Group."

"Bag it," Cohen said, and stood, extending the prize catch.

Cole double-wrapped the small machine in thick plastic bags and dropped it into the larger contraband sack Bangban was holding. McCoy put both hands on his hips.

"There goes two weeks of work," he sighed, and walked toward the hallway. "I know the drill, boys," he said, eschewing any assistance. Passing by, McCoy stomped his foot and both dogs slavered at the end of their tethers. McCoy laughed and disappeared down the hallway. Then the cops disassembled his quarters.

BACK IN THE nurses' station, the room sweeps over, the search teams relaxed. The police laid out their cache of extirpated goods on the work counter and carefully snapped a photo of each.

For a locked psychiatric unit behind an enormous fence, guarded by a maximum-security sally port, a surprising array of smuggled items had somehow found their way onto Unit C.

The officers took pictures of Caruthers's Sharpie pen and McCoy's tattoo machine—"They use the insides of a DVD player," Xiang said. From the envelope unearthed by the dogs came three Wellbutrin pills, a popular antidepressant prized by patients for crushing and snorting, and six OxyContin tablets—Mathews's "cheeked" narcotic pain reliever. The diminutive flask of spirits was photographed and, lastly, fourteen cigarettes.

"They go for ten dollars each," Xiang said.

Then we got to the shanks. In addition to the altered eyeglass stem, the room-squeeze had uncovered an oblong shard of jagged bathroom window glass with a rag handle and a small filed-edge screwdriver.

The assembled group fell quiet for a moment. "*Shank* is an ugly word," I said, and picked up the screwdriver.

"Technically that's not a shank," Cohen said. "A shank is any crudely fashioned, sharpened weapon," he continued. "Made from an otherwise nonimposing object, like the eyeglass stem, contrived for the purpose of stabbing. The screwdriver is inherently dangerous, not homemade or improvised, and thus not a shank."

The staff and cops turned his way.

"The word comes from the metal piece that connected the heel to the arch of old prison boots," Cohen continued. "That's called the shank. Prisoners would open the boots, take it out, and sharpen it."

"How do you know all this?" I asked as the cops turned back to finish up.

But Cohen had already walked away.

After the police tagged and cataloged the confiscated items, they checked a final time with Xiang, then ambled down the empty hall.

"Good to see you, Doc," Cole boomed, and waved from the door. From his scuffle with Mathews, one cheek looked swollen. I caught his eye and pointed to my own cheek. Cole grinned. "Worth it," he said, then Kate Henry let the cops out.

In an hour, the treatment team re-collected and confronted Mr. Smith about his gambling operation.

"Night shift said they caught you running a dice game," Xiang said.

"That's bullshit," Smith huffed.

"You're confined to the unit for one week," Xiang stated.

"Fuck you."

"Mr. Smith, what did we learn to do in group when things like this happen?" Palanqui said.

"Fuck you, too."

CHAPTER SIX

One side of me says, "I'd like to talk to her and date her." The other side says, "I wonder what her head would look like on a stick?"

—Edmund Kemper, who killed two grandparents by age fifteen. During the 1970s, he murdered and dismembered six female hitchhikers near Santa Cruz, California. He next killed his mother and her friend. Kemper is noted for his imposing size—six feet, nine inches—and his high IQ: 145.

"Let's get you an office," Kate Henry said after our visit with Smith. I grabbed some patient charts and followed.

We left the unit and walked down the long main corridor. She opened one door in a series and handed me the keys. "Any questions, don't hesitate to ask," she added.

Jail-cell small, the Spartan room contained a single grimy window that wouldn't open and a 1940s vintage metal desk and chair. On top of the desk sat a historical relic of a computer. A dented wastebasket completed the decor.

I piled the charts on my desk, then sat down and started the computer. In a rare nod to modernity, Gomorrah had recently instituted an electronic ordering system. I clicked on the Physician Orders tab and requisitioned a sitter for Cervantes.

A sitter is a staff member assigned to watch a dangerous patient and keep them from hurting themselves or anyone else. The sitter goes everywhere the patient goes; sitters rotate shifts, 24/7, until the emergency is over, usually two or three days. They're called sitters because they sit in a chair outside the patient's room and watch through the open door. It's a valuable service: sitters save lives.

I attempted to order some blood tests using a separate software program, which thwarted me at every turn. A dismissive pop-up that read "error" appeared repeatedly. Frustrated, I shut down the machine and headed outside to clear my head.

The hallway was filled with patients. Startled, I was engulfed in a wave of hungry psychopaths on their way to the cafeteria for lunch at the other end of the long hall.

People are usually surprised to learn that patients and staff at Gomorrah aren't separated. Patients live in unguarded double rooms like in any other hospital. They mix freely with the staff in open hallways. And while the unit door is locked, patients are frequently escorted out: for medical appointments in town, to see relatives in the visitors' center, for treatment groups in another building, or to visit the library across campus.

When patients walk to the dining hall and back, they share the same space as the staff going to and from their offices. It's dangerous, especially if there are stragglers. These are the people you meet face-to-face, often with no one else nearby.

Quickly retreating to my office, I wrote patient notes, then read charts until my eyes crossed. By three o'clock I'd never felt so drained.

I stood up and hit the hallway again. It was empty. I walked to the main entrance, unlocked the door, and headed outside. Ten feet down the sidewalk, an unyielding peacock confronted me.

I shooed him away, but he dug in. I tried again. He raised his head, shrieked toward the sky, and shot his stiletto beak at my right foot.

"Hey!" I said, and hopped aside. He reared and fired again. I jumped back and nearly reached for my personal alarm.

It was a low point. Coming to my senses, I left the device untouched, noted that, up close, peacocks are far larger than you might imagine, and scuttled back inside.

I'd just made it back to my office door when an alarm rang. I joined Cohen and a crowd that surged toward Unit C, where another battle had begun.

"Stupid bitch!" Mathews yelled as three staff members hustled him toward the restraint room. Luella sat on the floor, forehead resting on bent knees, blood dripping from her nose.

The extra staff and cops herded patients into the courtyard. The day shift surrounded Luella. Palanqui brought a pile of paper towels, took one in hand, and gently pressed it to both sides of Luella's nose. Luella looked like a deer caught in truck headlights. Her eyes saucers, her breathing rapid, she mumbled something in Spanish.

"What happened?" I asked Xiang. On his knees beside Luella, his arm cradled her shoulder.

"Luella told Mr. Mathews it's time for afternoon medication," Xiang said, and tried to control the emotion in his voice. "He turned and punched her in the face."

"Wasn't Mathews in restraints?" Cohen asked as I knelt next to Luella as well.

"We let him out after two hours," Xiang said. "He said he was calm."

"That's crazy," Cohen said. "He fought with a cop."

"You tell the people in administration," Xiang said. "Patients stay in restraints too long, I lose my job."

I gently pulled the now crimson-stained paper towel off Luella's nose, which was colored a deep black-purple and misshapen. I looked closely at Luella's eyes.

Bleeding into the eye can cause blindness. Intraocular blood produces a tiny crescent of fresh red between the inside lower edge of the cornea and the iris, the colored part of your eye. I looked closely. I didn't see any blood.

But when I asked Luella to "follow my finger," her right eye didn't move sideways. This usually signaled an orbital rim fracture, a break in one of the bones that surrounds your eye and in which a nerve or muscle has become trapped. Orbital rim fractures are serious business.

I felt Luella's neck and checked the integrity of the muscles in her face and tongue. Any distress there could mean neck or spinal cord injury.

"We'll get you looked at right away," I said, and gently assisted Luella to her feet. Still in shock, she was unsteady. We helped her to a chair Randy brought from the conference room. I touched Luella's arm and said, "I'm so sorry."

A paramedic crew loaded Luella onto a gurney and rolled her out the unit door, headed toward County General.

"How bad is it?" Xiang asked me nervously. Cohen was in earshot.

"Her nose is broken," I said. "And she's probably got an orbital rim fracture. Her right eye didn't move laterally. Either a nerve or muscle is trapped. She might need surgery to free it up."

"Oh my!" Xiang sighed.

Cohen looked ready to explode.

"I have no more nurses," Xiang said. "Twelve nurses, half our staff, got assaulted and are out on injury leave. We can't get more pool nurses. They refuse to come here."

"Nurses aren't stupid," Larsen huffed. "Who'd volunteer to come here? What's it worth to get your face broken?"

"You're here," Cohen said.

"So are you," Larsen countered.

Cohen didn't reply.

"Call the jerks in administration," Larsen continued. "Maybe they'll drop down and cover a shift or two. Let them take the next punch. Better yet, call Sacramento. Get the governor. I'll be first in line to sock him."

After that day, I expected a total collapse. But I was surprised to find that gradually everyone's raw emotions and anger were tamped back down. In fact, I would see this happen many times in the next few months. After days that a normal human shouldn't be able to tolerate, our staff repeatedly did something incredible: they returned to work. Slowly at first, and then at a normal pace, "regular" life on Unit C would start up again.

I walked to my office and stared out the grime-encrusted window. It looked onto an old enclosed patient courtyard that housed the remains of a raised-bed garden. The six planter boxes had long ago fallen into weedy disrepair. A solitary peacock pecked at the barren dirt.

I can't recall how long I stood at that window, but it was far past time to leave when I remembered my promise to speak with Mr. Caruthers. But I wasn't in any condition. The sun had set. I needed to go home. Locking my office, I said good night to Cohen, who was walking by.

Near the exit door, I turned to see the Unit C patients heading to the cafeteria for dinner. Among the throng, followed by a sitter, Cervantes and Hong walked hand in hand. Mathews, hale and chipper, spoke amiably with Boudreaux. NPR-man brought up the rear.

"That's all the news from Lake Wobegon," NPR-man said, and ducked into the dining hall.

I got out my keys, put one in the lock, and startled when a clang rang out. Turning, I saw a metal cafeteria tray rattle onto the floor. It had been thrown through the open dining hall doorway and crashed into the opposite corridor window. Eric, the swing shift tech, walked out, gathered up the tray, and marched resolutely back inside.

I followed, ready to bolster the staff forces, but it was apparent the trouble had ended. I stood near the doorway and listened. The only sound was the click of utensils and soft conversation.

I paced back to the exit door, casting a nervous glance down toward the cafeteria, and waited a few minutes in the hallway to be certain everything remained quiet.

When I was certain there was no further trouble, I undid the main door lock and headed out. Dark as pitch, the night hung heavy and moonless.

I crossed the front grass and had gone a few steps down the main road when I spied something out of the corner of my eye. I stopped and turned. By the light from a tall streetlamp, just inside the perimeter fence and below a sign that read "Out of Bounds," two figures stood behind the Unit C building, outlined against the darkness.

The shadowy pair, their heads cloaked in dark hoodies, cast furtive glances from side to side, but neither appeared to notice me.

One person held out a carton of cigarettes, which the other person quickly took and hid beneath his shirt. The second person produced a fistful of cash and put it into the first person's hands. Both figures disappeared behind the building.

I froze, uncertain what to do. Fearing I still might be seen, I attempted to remain calm, then started to walk away. After ten paces I broke into a run and didn't stop until I hit the sally port.

After I bent to catch my breath, I looked back down the empty main road and decided that whatever would come of this sighting, it would have to come in the light of day. Wiping sweat from my forehead, I turned in my alarm and keys and retraced my path back through the labyrinthine entry system. Leaving the hospital grounds brought much less scrutiny than entering. I flashed my ID badge into a reader at each port and the gates buzzed open.

The parking lot was dimly lit and nearly empty. Attached to the fence by baling wire, a solitary bulb shone onto my truck and two other adjacent cars. At my vehicle door, I fumbled for my keys.

"What kind of crazy place is this?" a voice said out of the darkness.

It was Cohen.

CHAPTER SEVEN

Mental illness can happen to anybody. You can be a dustman, a politician, a Tesco worker . . . anyone. It could be your dad, your brother or your aunt.

—Frank Bruno, British boxer and former WBC Heavyweight World Champion. Suffers from bipolar disorder.

At home, after a late dinner, I was firmly in an alternate universe. The one from my previous life. The one from two days ago. We had a pleasant meal and then watched two episodes of *Portlandia,* a recent favorite of John's.

Getting ready for bed, I stood beside Ingrid and looked at our reflections in the vanity mirror. She slowly brushed her blond hair.

"What is it?" Ingrid said quietly.

I didn't know where to start. But I knew Ingrid didn't need to hear about Luella getting her face smashed. Or Cervantes threatening to stab me. Or the shakedown. The shanks. The patients in the hallway. But I needed to talk about something.

"Dr. Cohen, my psychologist, and I were the last staff persons to leave the unit building," I said.

"He's the one you met during orientation?" Ingrid asked.

I nodded. "He left ahead of me. There was a little dust-up in the cafeteria and I ran over, but it was nothing. Then I left as well. Outside, just beyond the fence lights, I saw two people behind the unit building."

"The police?" Ingrid asked.

"They weren't police," I said. "One person passed a carton of cigarettes to the other and received money in return. Then they ducked away. No one is supposed to be behind the unit buildings. Ever." I waited for Ingrid's response.

"And . . . ?" she said simply.

"And when I got to the car," I continued, "I ran into Dr. Cohen again."

"So . . . ?"

"He might have been one of the people I saw behind the building," I said, glad to finally have it out. "I don't think he expected to see me."

"If one of those people was Dr. Cohen," Ingrid said, "how did he get to the parking lot ahead of you?"

I thought for a moment. "I don't know. You're right. That place is crazy and it's making me crazy."

Sleep proved difficult. I turned one way, then the other, and back again a dozen times. Finally I sat on the side of the bed, checked the clock—it was nearly midnight—and went to the study.

I pulled a psychiatric textbook off a shelf and sat down to read. Knowledge is power and right then I needed some empowerment. I needed to know why Gomorrah was the way it was.

THE PROBLEM OF mental illness and crime goes back to the dawn of recorded history. The Code of Hammurabi, the ancient Mesopotamian rules, the world's first written system of law, forbade the punishment of insane persons for crimes. Down through the ages, every society in one fashion or another has followed this credo.

There have been numerous iterations of the so-called insanity defense in both American and British law. I read through long, convoluted explanations of the McNaughton rules, the irresistible impulse test, the Durham rule, and, finally, the American Law Institute Model Penal Code test.

I concluded that Ben Cohen's summary of the insanity defense had been basically correct. "Not guilty by reason of insanity" means you were crazy when you committed the crime, and "incompetent to stand trial" means you're crazy when you come up for trial. Either way you get sent for medical treatment instead of prison.

A third legal classification comprises convicts who go crazy in prison. On their release date, if the person is deemed dangerous because of a mental illness, we get them as well. They're called mentally disordered offenders (MDO), and while not strictly an insanity defense issue, they're a growing population in state hospitals.

Despite extensive press coverage, the insanity defense is successfully employed only 25 percent of the time. But the potential for abuse is obvious: you kill someone, then claim you were crazy, or high on drugs or alcohol or Twinkies. These scams shouldn't work. But sometimes they do. There were patients on Unit C, I would learn, who'd dodged the hangman and lied their way in.

This last group, the scammers, is included under the larger heading of antisocial personality disorder (ASPD). Here *antisocial* doesn't mean they're loners who don't mix well. It means they won't follow the social laws of society; i.e., they won't stop robbing, murdering, and raping people.

ASPD persons are schemers and opportunists; they sense and

then take advantage of weakness. They're wheeler-dealers, people who buy and sell drugs, stolen goods, and guns. They run protection rings: you pay money or get beat up. They're involved in prostitution, gambling, and smuggling. They frequently get into fights.

They're also called con men. The "con" part is short for "confidence." These people use their considerable skills at manipulation to gain the trust of others, whom they then exploit. Persons with ASPD are also called sociopaths. These are the career criminals of the world. People with ASPD make up 50 to 75 percent of state prison populations.

I didn't have to read much about ASPD. I'd dealt with those people for years. They bedevil the psychiatric cosmos. ASPD persons aren't mentally ill but can mimic it very convincingly. Gomorrah housed a small but real number of strictly ASPD cases, people who'd conned a judge and attorney into believing they were sick, as apparently McCoy had done.

Often faced with long prison terms or lethal injection, these people pretend to be crazy. Randle Patrick McMurphy, Jack Nicholson's character in *One Flew Over the Cuckoo's Nest*, wasn't mentally ill. He had ASPD.

Adding to the difficulty of Gomorrah, many of our patients have both ASPD *and* mental illness. They are psychotic sociopaths, the psychopaths you hear about, which helps explain the often bizarre and grisly nature of some crimes. Sociopaths will perpetrate a stock fraud, steal your wallet, or shoot you during a botched drug deal. Psychopaths slice you into small pieces because God told them to. Sociopaths and psychopaths comprise a significant proportion of patients at Gomorrah, which is one reason it's such a difficult and dangerous place.

It was two a.m. before I closed the text, slid it back onto the shelf, and returned to bed.

CHAPTER EIGHT

"Well, Clarice—have the lambs stopped screaming?"

—Hannibal Lecter, *The Silence of the Lambs*

The next morning, sleep deprived, fighting a gnawing sense of dread, I showered and dressed. Ingrid had risen early to pedal the exercise bike we'd parked in front of the living room TV. I snagged my hospital ID, truck keys, and wallet from a side table in the hall. John had just begun to stir.

Ingrid stood beside me, glistening, a rolled towel around her neck. "I know you didn't sleep much," she said. "Tell me if you need anything."

I kissed her on the cheek and waved at John, who'd emerged into the hallway. He braved a smile and signaled back groggily.

In the driveway, I started my car and looked toward the front window of the house. A finger parted the curtains, and the thin profile of John's face appeared. "I love you," I mouthed, and pointed to him. The curtain closed. Punching the radio dial, I pulled into the street.

It was silent when I stopped by my office and walked to Unit C. After unlocking the door, I strode down an empty unit hallway, joined Xiang and the others on their way to the conference room, and took my seat at the shaky table.

I still felt overwhelmed. Or tongue-tied. Or something. But I didn't say anything about Cervantes's threat or the cigarettes. Or ask about Luella.

"Where'd all the patients go?" I asked instead.

"In their rooms," Xiang replied. "Everyone's very quiet. We know something is happening. This is just a distraction. The main event is coming up."

"What main event?" I asked.

"I hear someone on Unit B, probably Mike Morgan, has a bone to pick with one of our patients," Palanqui said.

"Mr. Morgan is a troubled soul," added Virginia Hancock, a new nurse—white, middle-aged. "He lived here on Unit C a while back. We all remember Mr. Morgan."

"We haven't met," I said. "I'm Dr. Seager."

"Ms. Hancock worked here for many years," Xiang said. "She's just back from six months on leave. With Luella out, we were very lucky to find her."

"Nice to meet you," I said. "Welcome back."

"Glad to be back," Hancock replied. "And nice to meet you."

"Mr. Morgan is a major wheeler-dealer," Xiang added, steering us back on topic.

"He can hook you up with whatever you need," Monabong said. "You doctors need anything?"

Cohen shook his head. "I'm good. But thanks for asking."

"If you change your mind," Monabong went on, "Morgan can get drugs, pruno, cigarettes, food; he's got a finger in everything."

"What's pruno?" I asked.

"Home-brewed prison alcohol," Palanqui interjected. "They ferment fruit cocktail from the cafeteria."

"Fermented fruit cocktail?" Cohen put a finger in his mouth and performed a gagging pantomime.

"You don't mess with Mr. Morgan," Xiang said. "He has henchmen everywhere. You have trouble with him, you're going to get it."

"The target's probably Mr. Mathews," Larsen said. "My sources say they had a little squabble last week down at the patient commissary."

"You have 'sources'?" I asked.

"People tell us things," Xiang stated.

"I'm guessing that information doesn't come cheap," Cohen said. Xiang didn't respond.

From the hallway Mathews suddenly shouted, "Don't fuck with me, white boy!"

"Fuck you!" an equally loud voice replied. Mayhem exploded: banging, cursing, and the sickening thwack of fists crashing into faces. I was too terrified to move. But not the rest of the team.

"Showtime," Xiang said, and pushed his hip alarm, adding sirens and lights to the chaos. Everyone, Cohen included, rose to their feet. Xiang opened the door and they shot out into the fray.

From what well of courage these people drew their strength remained a mystery. I didn't have any of it. I stood frozen at the door, stunned by the violence. Cohen had joined in like a seasoned veteran. The entire unit, it seemed, was beating one another.

Mathews, blood cascading from his nose, squared off against Shawn Carver, a huge young white man, his left eye nearly closed from a mass the size of an egg on his cheekbone. Xiang and Hancock had wrestled Boudreaux to the ground. Near their feet, Cohen had been thrown to the floor and began to rise. A trio of staff corralled Cervantes and Hong, bustling them to safety, then they ran back and tossed themselves into the tangle of flailing arms and kicking legs.

Mathews landed a looping right hand onto Carver's other cheek. Carver reeled as if drunk, collected his balance, recoiled, and swung back. A boulder-sized fist mashed Mathews square on the jaw and he dropped.

Xiang and the nurses disentangled from everyone else, surrounded Carver, cocooned his limbs with theirs—Lilliputians to Gulliver—and rode him to the linoleum.

Mathews, face on the tile, blood dripping off his chin, pushed a knee beneath himself and bellowed. Cohen caught my eye. And for reasons I still can't explain, in tandem, we rushed forward, knocked Mathews sideways, and fell into a jumbled heap. I grabbed an arm and hung on for dear life. After an eternity, someone yanked my shirt collar and pulled me free. It was Cole. Behind him stood Bangban.

Despite the presence of hospital police, the brawl continued. An older man jumped onto Bangban's back and beat the top of his head with balled fists. Xiang peeled him away. The cops finally subdued Mathews and wrangled him toward the restraint room.

Xiang and Cohen lifted a stunned Carver onto his feet and plastered him against a door frame. Xiang deactivated his hip alarm and the blaring siren fell silent; the flashing lights clicked off. Spent, everyone relaxed for a second.

In that instant, with a sudden spasm of Herculean strength, Carver flexed away from his captors, ripped a shard of sharpened metal from his sock, and tore after Mathews. Everyone froze except

Xiang, who spun and charged Carver, ramming him full force, waist high, and planting him into the nearest wall. With a swipe, Xiang crashed Carver's hand into a door frame and the shank jangled to the floor.

Xiang pulled an arm, rolled his hip, and jujitsu whipped Carver to the ground. The cops once again covered the fallen man. I dashed over and grabbed the shank. It was a filed door hinge.

Inside of ten minutes everything on Unit C had returned to normal. Sedated, Carver and Mathews lay in restraints. I'd checked them both for any neurological damage or facial trauma. After they'd calmed sufficiently, X-rays had been ordered.

The staff had ensconced all the other patients in their rooms. The cops photographed and cataloged Carver's shank. The same pair of janitors mopped and disinfected the floor. The staff stood in the nurses' station and washed up.

"How'd we miss that shank during the shakedown?" Cohen asked.

"I wonder what else we missed," I added.

"We missed seeing McCoy during the fight," Cohen said.

"Mr. McCoy is too smart," Xiang said, and rinsed his face. "He only picks the fights he knows he can win."

Xiang briefly inspected a swollen cheek in the mirror, then returned to a spot behind the station computer, which he clicked on. Cohen, Kate Henry, and I watched the scene.

"That man is something else," Cohen said.

"Amen to that," Kate Henry concurred.

Before leaving the unit, I caught Hancock's attention. We stood near the nurses' station door. She rubbed her shoulder.

"Are you hurt?" I asked.

"It's nothing," Hancock replied.

"May I ask you a question?" I said.

"Sure."

"Were you injured here at work? Is that why you went on leave?"

"Six months ago," Hancock said, "during a patient takedown, I tore the rotator cuff in my shoulder."

"I'm sorry to hear that," I said. "But you're okay now?"

"Good as can be expected," Hancock said, and grinned.

I smiled back. "Will you allow me another question?"

"Of course."

"Why did you come back?"

Hancock didn't reply for a moment. "Before I answer, may I ask you a question?"

"Shoot."

"Are you a religious person?"

"I was born in Utah," I said, uncertain where we were headed. "I come from a religious background."

"I call working here a 'Jesus job,'" Hancock said. "I often ask people, if you knew Jesus was coming back for a day and you wanted to find him, where would you go?"

I looked out the station window. Burns slowly wheeled by in his chair, gesturing frantically and mumbling to himself.

"Who else would care for them?" Hancock asked. She patted my arm and walked out the door.

I thought for a moment about what Hancock said. Then I suddenly remembered a loose end: I needed to track down Tom Caruthers.

He sat alone on a couch in the dayroom, a large on-unit communal area where patients congregated for conversation, board games, or to watch TV. The television was tuned to Fox News.

"Mr. Caruthers," I said, and stepped inside. "May we go down the hall and talk?"

"You promised we'd speak Tuesday," he said, not moving.

"I'm sorry," I replied. "Things just got so crazy. . . ."

Caruthers turned from the TV and stood. I stepped back. I'd forgotten how tall he was.

"You didn't stick up for me during the shakedown," he spat, and edged forward.

My hand drew near my belt alarm. "Again, I'm sorry," I said.

Caruthers paused. "What do you want to talk about?" he finally sighed. His mercurial temperament had tipped downward toward depression. This was his pattern. Caruthers suffered from what's called rapid cycling bipolar disorder, an illness typified by mood swings in faster succession than standard bipolar disorder. A person can careen from high to low and back in a single day or even an hour. I knew he'd have to be monitored closely. In the past, these volatile whipsaws had produced suicidal thoughts.

"Let's go down to the conference room," I suggested.

"Okay," Caruthers said. "And you can take your hand away from the alarm."

Caruthers and I took posts on opposite sides of the conference room table. Seeing him again roused the same feelings I'd experienced two decades ago. I didn't see Caruthers as a grown man. He was once again the terrified teenager so distraught and in need of comfort. Rather than a patient, I saw an old friend. Perhaps a grown son.

"Tell me what happened that you had to come here," I said.

Caruthers paused. "I got married, Doc," he began, and his mood barometer rose. Easing into a casual tone, we slowly settled back two decades. "What a mistake. For years that woman was nothing but trouble. You know the kind of misery a certain sort of woman can bring into a man's life?"

"I can imagine," I said.

"Anyway," Caruthers went on, "one day, like she did, she started to drink around noon and pretty soon her mouth was motoring full on. And that lady could cuss. You never heard such words. We fought all day. By evening things got real ugly. I mean personal and ugg-lee. And then, I remember the moment clearly—it was ten twenty-three on the kitchen clock—after all those years and all the crap she'd dished out, I knew I'd finally had enough. So I killed her. Hit her in the head with a two-by-four, then cut her up with a butcher knife, bagged everything in plastic trash sacks, and threw them in the trunk of my car." He shook his head. "Can you believe it?"

I stared at Caruthers, unable to reply. His tale had shaken me out of my torpor. This wasn't a terrified teenager. Caruthers was a killer.

"A week later I was flying high and got stopped for running a red light," Caruthers continued, unfazed. "There was an odor. The cops opened the trunk. And here I am."

"Were you taking your medication?" I asked feebly.

"Hell no, Doc," Caruthers said. "You know how nutty I get when I don't take my meds. But that's not the crazy part."

"What's the crazy part?" I said, horrified. My feelings toward Caruthers had always been complicated, but now I didn't have the right word to describe them.

"Since I came here," Caruthers said, "I quit drinking and doing drugs. I have a job with the grounds crew. I play basketball every Sunday and run three times a week. I'm in the best shape of my life. I'm involved in unit government. My steady girl lives over in the A wing. Hell," he continued, and opened his hands, "if I knew I'd get sent to a place like this, I'd have killed that woman ten years before."

CHAPTER NINE

I had officially joined the cacophony of sick motherfuckers.

—Betsy Lerner, *Food and Loathing: A Life Measured Out in Calories*

I walked into rounds on Friday morning and knew the time had arrived. I'd planned to speak with Cohen first but realized that was just postponing the inevitable.

"When I left work last Tuesday night," I said after the team had taken their seats, "I saw something go on behind the unit building. I should have spoken up earlier."

"What happened?" Xiang said.

"Someone sold a carton of cigarettes to another person."

"Did a patient buy them?" Palanqui asked.

"Could have been. It was dark," I replied.

"Very serious," Xiang said. "We'll notify the hospital police right away."

"Did you see who sold them?" Cohen asked. I couldn't read his face.

"They stood in the shadows of the fence lights," I replied. "Just out of sight."

"I left late that night as well," Cohen said. "Remember, we met in the parking lot?" I nodded. "I didn't see anything," Cohen went on. "But that stuff happens. Contraband gets in here somehow."

"I'll notify hospital police," Kate Henry said. "Please, no one speak about this to anyone. Let the authorities handle it."

"No problem," I said.

"Of course," Randy added.

Rounds proceeded as if nothing had happened. It was a skill I would quickly learn to employ myself.

"Is it just me," I said in the nurses' station that afternoon, "or is there an odd vibe on the unit today?"

Cohen nodded toward a group of patients passing by on their way to the courtyard. Chatting casually, they smiled. McCoy followed and gave us a wave.

"Notice anything strange?" Xiang asked.

"They're not bashing each other in the face?" Cohen offered.

"They've got Bibles," Xiang said. "That's a bad sign."

"What's the problem with Bibles?" I asked.

"Everyone has one," Xiang replied. "The men hide all sorts of bad shit in there."

"Opiates, the religion of the masses," Cohen interjected.

"Once a month the hospital has Friday-night church service," Xiang said. "Patients from all the units attend. Very big deal."

"You think something bad is going down at church?" I asked.

"Always does," Palanqui said. "Drug deals, beatings, sex, money, cigarettes. The usual."

"This happens at church?" I asked.

The staff looked at me like I was an idiot.

"Wow," Cohen deadpanned. "That's a bad church."

"Can't we just stop it?" I asked. "And why doesn't someone search the Bibles before they leave the unit?"

The staff veterans shared a knowing look.

"Friday-night church is the most important event of the month," Xiang said. "We stop that, we get riots for sure."

"The Patient Rights Department says searching a Bible violates a person's privacy rights," Monabong said. "We search Bibles, they'd be all over our ass. We'd be filling out forms till the day we die."

"So what do we do?" I asked.

"What can we do?" Xiang said.

Apparently having forgotten something, McCoy retraced his route. By the nurses' station he stopped, clasped the Bible to his chest, and looked heavenward. Then he roared with laughter and continued on.

"Someday he'll screw up," Xiang said quietly.

"Then we'll see who's laughing," Cohen added.

Later that afternoon in my office I got a call from the unit.

"Detective Levin is here to see you," Xiang said.

I was busy writing my daily notes on a dozen charts. "Can he come to my office?"

Xiang paused. "He says no. You come here."

"What's this about?" I said, but Xiang had hung up the phone.

I walked to the unit, nervously jangling keys in my pocket, then entered the nurses' station.

"Dr. Seager?" said a tall, crew-cut man in a white short-sleeved shirt, gray pants, and tie. I looked at his footwear. I'd heard the term *cop shoes* but had never really seen any. Black oxfords with worn heels and round toes probably hiding steel covers, a bit too shiny: cop shoes.

"I'm Detective Levin," the man said, and we shook hands.

"What's this about?" I asked.

"Let's go back to the conference room," Levin said, and we headed out. He knew right where to go.

We took seats on opposite sides of the wooden table. Like Sergeant Joe Friday on *Dragnet*, Levin pulled a small notebook and stubby pencil from a shirt pocket. "We understand you saw a staff member sell a carton of cigarettes to a patient," he began.

"Last Tuesday night, out behind Unit C," I said. "I saw someone who might have been a staff member sell what looked like a carton of cigarettes to someone else," I replied.

"You said it was a staff member," Levin countered. I didn't like his tone.

"I don't know who it was. It could have been a staff member."

Levin riffled back through his diminutive pad. He held a page at arm's length and used his pencil for a pointer. "Says here 'staff member,'" he said. "Are you changing your story?"

My heart skipped. "What? I haven't talked to anybody about this. Kate Henry called you."

Levin looked puzzled but remained silent. He was good. If I'd been guilty I might have cracked.

Finally Levin relented. "Seems you're right. It does mention Ms. Henry." I relaxed. "Did you tell Ms. Henry you saw a staff member sell cigarettes to a patient?"

I snapped to attention again. "It doesn't matter what I said to whom. I saw someone sell what looked like a carton of cigarettes to someone else behind Unit C."

"Any description of either person?" Levin said in a matter-of-fact tone, and for the next fifteen minutes I gave as detailed a report as possible. Levin jotted down the salient points. Then he closed the little book and we stood. I shook his extended hand.

"You think of anything else," Levin said, "or see anything else—or if anyone talks to you about this—call me."

"I will," I said, uncomfortable with the great relief I felt. And then a thought hit me.

"Do you know our patient, Mr. McCoy?" I asked.

"Huge man. *HELL* tattooed across his forehead," Levin said. "Beat another patient with a chair."

"Is he going to face charges?"

Levin paused. "The matter's under investigation," he said, and stepped to the exit.

Levin half opened the conference room door, then turned. "One more thing," he added. "You know this cigarette business is a felony. A person could lose their job and maybe do jail time."

"I know now," I replied.

"Police work is funny," Levin said with a disarming smile. "Sometimes the person who pulls the alarm started the fire."

Before I could reply, Levin walked out the door.

MY FIRST WEEK was over. Saturday morning, as Ingrid and I took a bike ride on a nearby mountain trail, she asked me about my job. We pulled over, dismounted, and sat on the ground.

"I think everyone at Gomorrah is insane," I began. "The staff's just as nutty as the patients. You should see these people. They jump into fights with the convicts or patients or whatever they're called like it's nothing. In the hallway two huge men are smashing each other with their fists. Blood is everywhere. I can't move. But the entire unit staff—nurses, therapists, my psychologist—all dive right in. Mr. Xiang, the head nurse, took down the biggest one."

Ingrid had a look of horror on her face. I'd seen it only a few times before. "I didn't mean to . . ." I said.

"I'm all right," Ingrid replied. "Is there more?"

I let it out. The shakedown. The shanks. The crimes. The fights. Mathews and Carver. The gore. The terror. McCoy. Caruthers ("He's okay—I guess the murderers you know are better than the ones you don't"). The computer. My office. Kate Henry. Management. Dr. Tom. Xiang. Ben Cohen. "And a peacock tried to stab my foot," I said. "Every day is like real-life Mortal Kombat. It's just crazy dangerous."

"Is that it?" Ingrid said.

"Isn't that enough?" I hadn't mentioned the death threat from Cervantes, the battering of Luella, or Detective Levin's veiled insinuation. I'd barely allowed myself to think about them.

"Way enough."

Ingrid didn't speak for a while. "You haven't slept all week," she finally began. "John's upset. Even the dogs are tense."

"I noticed they've been off," I said.

Ingrid stood, paced a few steps, and gazed down into the valley. "Why do you go back? Why work in such an awful place?" she asked.

"We need the money."

"This isn't about money," Ingrid said, and turned. "I don't know what it's about, but it's not money. Nobody puts up with that for money."

I took a moment.

"I've never been in a situation like this," I said. "I'd hate to leave the team. I'm just getting to know them and they seem really good. And the unit really needs a doctor. . . ." My voice trailed.

"I love you and I want to be supportive," Ingrid said. "But it's not looking good right now."

"I understand."

Ingrid walked back to her bike and swung a leg over. "How about we give it two more weeks?" she said. "Is that fair?" She fastened her helmet's chin strap and pointed her bike down the hill.

"Two weeks," I replied.

"Unless Mr. Hell-on-His-Face pounds you senseless before then."

CHAPTER TEN

Night and day among the tombs . . . he was always crying and cutting himself with stones.

—Mark 5:5

Jesus then asked him, "What is your name?" And he said, "Legion," for many demons had entered him.

—Luke 8:30

Every so often an unusual thing happened on Unit C. The next two weeks were a near constant stream of chaos and alarms. We had a string of fights, a number of cafeteria flare-ups, and, most distressingly, Mr. Gomez, a notorious sex offender, grabbed Palanqui, held her against the nurses' station door, and attempted to pull down her pants. This caused a near brawl. The other patients were just as upset with Gomez as the staff was. They wanted to kill him.

Seriously shaken, Palanqui went home, but amazingly came back in two days. "No work, no money," she said at rounds on that second Thursday.

Xiang took the event badly. With him, a nurse getting hurt, physically or emotionally, was personal. He said nothing but was visibly distraught.

But then the unusual thing happened.

"Mr. McCoy, you're late for lunch," Xiang called into the unit hallway that afternoon as the patients repaired to the cafeteria.

"Sorry, thank you," McCoy said, and caught Xiang's eye. He struggled to pull on his baby-blue shirt, then trotted toward the unit door, which Randy held open.

After medication time on Friday morning, Mathews spied a stray pill on the floor. He bent, picked it up, and, holding the tablet between his fingers, presented it to Palanqui, who stood behind the small medication-room Dutch door.

"You dropped this," Mathews said, and placed the pellet in Palanqui's hand.

Later, Carver and Mathews bumped shoulders in the hallway. Behind the nurses' station window, I froze. But after a flash of electricity, Mathews said, "Sorry," and both went on their way.

After lunch, Boudreaux spoke with Randy in the hallway. "He invited me to watch the Giants game on TV tomorrow night," Randy said to me afterward. "They're playing the Dodgers. I never met anybody who knows more about baseball."

"Why is everyone being so nice?" I asked.

"I don't trust it," Cohen said. "These guys are professional schemers. Something's up. Something's always up."

Larsen had walked up behind us unnoticed. "These guys may be the lowest of the low," she said. "They've killed their parents or some kids, or raped a string of strangers—they've done things for which nothing could ever atone—but they're still human beings."

"If you've got a real low definition of *human being*," Cohen said.

"The patients and staff here at Gomorrah are locked in some kind of sick dance," Larsen continued. "You know that wave of helpless anxiety you feel when you walk onto the unit? The patients feel it, too. But they live here. They wake up in this nightmare. It's in their face twenty-four-seven."

Larsen looked at the floor. "You can't be frightened every minute of the day. So we each construct a story about why we started here and why we come back and why it's not so bad. And the patients construct similar stories. But when violence erupts, it shatters everyone's carefully built facade and we're faced again with that stark reality: we're all locked in this nuthouse together."

"I understand," Cohen added coolly, "the stark reality that these guys didn't get what they deserved." Cervantes and Hong passed by holding hands.

"No they didn't," Larsen said. "And coming to grips with that dilemma is important. Fairness doesn't really factor into the equation. It's pretty basic. Right or wrong, the state of California sent these men here for treatment and they pay us to render that treatment. We've all struck a bargain. They traded hospital for jail; we traded safety for money. And everyone just tries to get through the day as best they can.

"It all hinges on control," Larsen went on. "Everyone here—patients and staff—believes in the illusion of control. Violence exposes control for the fantasy it is. And that's what's so profoundly disturbing. The patients suffer just like us."

"For a day, maybe," Cohen said.

"True enough," Larsen replied. "But that's why Mathews returned the pill. Why Carver and he didn't fight. And why Boudreaux is focused on baseball. They want to reestablish the normal equilibrium."

Cohen took a moment, then turned to Larsen. "I still don't trust these guys," he said. "No matter what you say."

Larsen smiled. "I trust them as far as I can throw a piano," she stated, and walked out of the nurses' station door.

By Friday afternoon, Unit C had returned to normal. As the patients lined up for lunch, two frail men, Oliver Burns, a rail-thin, older black man, and Manuel Ortega, Caruthers's roommate, struggled to maneuver their wheelchairs into place. Burns inadvertently rolled over Carver's toe.

"What the fuck!" Carver yelped, then hopped on one foot and smacked Burns on the back of the head. Burns lurched forward and fell face-first onto the tile. He hit with a thud.

"Damn fool," Carver said, and angrily kicked Burns's chair away.

Enraged, Ortega grabbed his wheels, rocked back, then heaved forward and rammed his metal chair into Carver's knees, dropping Carver to the floor.

I pushed my alarm. Sirens erupted. A brief melee ensued. The staff broke it up and, surprisingly, tempers quickly cooled. Carver limped to the seclusion room; Xiang followed, a syringe ready. Cohen and I hoisted Burns back into his chair.

I tried to examine Burns, but he slapped my hand away. "I don't need nothin' but lunch," he snarled.

"Please let me . . ." I persisted.

Burns battered my arm even harder, seething. "Fuck you. Open the goddamn door. I'm hungry."

"We'll speak with Mr. Carver," Cohen said to Burns. "This won't happen again."

"Carver didn't do nothin'," Burns said. "I slipped out of my chair and fell on the floor. I'm fine. Now open the fucking door."

Sometimes I forgot that despite their age and the hospital clothes, the older patients were still convicts. And convicts don't rat one another out. I looked at Cohen, who looked back at me. Then I opened the door.

That night I left work late. I'd been hip deep in chart notes and decided to get them all finished. It was dark when I opened the unit door and stepped into the cool night air.

Walking the main road at night was a surreal experience. Being surrounded by bubbling psychosis and constant chaos, encircled by an impenetrable fence, made me claustrophobic. I hastened my pace.

And then my heart leaped. Halfway to the sally port, out of the murky gloaming behind me, a pair of car headlights sparked up. I turned but didn't stop walking. The car slowly pulled down the center drag but never fast enough to pass me. As it rolled under a streetlamp, I saw it was a police car.

Maybe it was being locked inside the fence or the stifling darkness, but the sight of that cop car made my skin crawl.

As I maintained a steady clip just beyond the headlights, I thought of Detective Levin and the carton of cigarettes.

The car trailed me all the way to the sally port, and when I stepped up onto the curb it turned, then slowly accelerated down a side road toward the Catholic chapel.

Once inside my truck, I fired the engine, took a deep breath, and looked in the rearview mirror. Beads of sweat ran down my forehead. I turned and gazed at the roll of razor wire atop the tall hospital fence. A bit of moonlight made it glint. It took a second to name my feeling: I was relieved to be on the outside.

CHAPTER ELEVEN

Okay, you guys, pair up in threes.

–Yogi Berra

Over the following weeks, I struggled with my conflicted feelings about Gomorrah and began operating on a sort of autopilot, hoping things would get better or that my decision to stay or leave would somehow be made for me. Then, inexplicably, I relaxed and actually began to inspect the place.

I looked more closely at the wheelchair patients, observing Ortega's struggle to navigate the crowded hallway and the difficulties Burns experienced maneuvering around the cafeteria. I started to understand how vulnerable they both were. I was terrified of Unit C, and I could run away. How much worse, I wondered, must it be for them?

I began to appreciate, amid the general ruckus, the many small acts of kindness that occurred. One morning I saw Hancock wheel Ortega away from the commotion as patients jostled and elbowed toward the unit door before breakfast. After everyone had surged by, I held the door as she maneuvered him safely toward the dining hall.

I watched Randy leave his work and wheel Burns down to lunch just before the line closed. Then Randy loped back to the nurses' station and continued on without a word.

One night I left late. In the hallway, I stopped at a conference room door and looked in the small lit window. Kate Henry sat with an older couple, a patient's family, I supposed, in a far corner of the large room. The woman cried quietly beside her clearly distraught husband. Kate Henry took the woman's hand and held it. The woman put her other hand on top of Kate Henry's and they sat silently.

I noticed, as well, lost in that blue sea of deluded and unbalanced persons, a number of elderly men. Skulking at the rear, they stood slump-shouldered and stared at the floor. Few, if any, ever spoke. You had to look to see them.

I knew many of these were the old-timers spoken about by Xiang. The folks who were just mentally ill. Those who'd come to Gomorrah before the fence was erected, before the criminals came. Before they were constantly surrounded by predators.

One older man in a wheelchair resembled my father. "Who's that?" I asked Xiang one day.

"Mr. Alvin Washington," Xiang replied. "He's been here longer than me. He's been here longer than anyone can remember. I think they built the place around him."

"He can't weigh more than ninety pounds. Is he safe here?" I asked.

"No one's safe here," Xiang said.

Most surprising, I realized that, despite being acutely aware of the awful things my patients had done, I had begun to feel affection for some of the murderers and rapists under my care.

Caruthers and I spoke frequently. Even with the terrible revelation of his murder, I found my old feelings for him creeping back, and we settled into a rhythm. Once or twice a week we sat and talked about what was going on with him. His feelings and his plans. "You mean when I get discharged?" he said with a grin. We reminisced about our time together at LA County. We talked about Gomorrah and the people we knew. We laughed. After a few weeks, we'd pretty much picked up where we left off.

Hong routinely smiled at me as I passed. Ortega said, "*Buenos días*," every morning. McCoy and I bumped knuckles each time we crossed in the hall. I can't recall how or why this ritual started, but it gradually became standard. We never talked about it. We just started doing it. I still kept Cervantes at arm's length, and though he never again approached me to speak, he still tapped his eyeglass frame when we passed each other, just to remind me what he had planned.

Some of the older men, like Burns and Washington, and most of the seriously ill schizophrenics didn't appear much on my radar. They stayed to themselves and declined to speak even if I asked. Except for meals, they rarely left their rooms. The staff ticked their names off at rounds, I kept an eye on their medical conditions and psychiatric medications, but they wouldn't allow much else.

NPR-man was his usual self. He zoomed around with seemingly unbounded energy. "All things considered," he'd said at the end of every sentence for the past month.

And I got to know Raymond Boudreaux better. When not infused with spells of psychotic rage, he was a sophisticated, pleasant man.

"You enjoy music, Doc?" he asked one afternoon as we crossed paths. I had a momentary pang recalling our first meeting.

"I do," I said, and stopped.

"How about New Orleans jazz?" he asked. "Not Dixieland jazz. There's a difference, you know."

I didn't, but said I did.

"If you want real New Orleans jazz—not that Pete Fountain commercial junk—I mean the real thing," Boudreaux continued, "you come down. I'll take you to Peter Street and we'll hear the Preservation Hall Band."

"The older guys," I said.

"All the old folks have passed now," Boudreaux said. "Sweet Emma Barrett, Kid Thomas Valentine, they're gone. But a new group keeps coming up. And they stay true to the basics."

"That sounds terrific," I said. "Thanks for the offer."

Boudreaux nodded and we went our separate ways.

Despite all this, when it came down to it, I was still more frightened of Gomorrah than anything else. I may have known my patients better, and my feelings may have softened, but the sound of fists hitting faces and the sight of Wilkins's brains on the floor still trumped everything else.

COHEN AND I had lunch one afternoon.

"I'm trying to sort through my feelings about this place," I said. We sat at a metal picnic table just outside the fence and opened a bag of Mexican food we'd purchased from a truck at the curb across the green. "I've contemplated quitting. My wife thinks I should. But I don't know. What's your experience?"

"I like it here," Cohen said and unwrapped a burrito. "I know that makes me a freak, but I can't help it. When I leave here I feel awake. The air is cleaner. My food tastes better. Hell, even sex is better. I know this sounds stupid, but I've never felt more alive in my life."

"You're right, you are a freak," I said, surprised by Cohen's statement. I didn't feel anything like that.

Driving home, I reviewed my conversation with Cohen, rehashed the events since I'd started working at Gomorrah, then tried to inventory my feelings and, finally, to think about the future. When I thought about staying at my job, my pulse quickened; when I thought about leaving, it returned to normal. My decision seemingly made, I decided to finally lay things out with Ingrid and admit that I planned to quit. I even tried out a few opening lines.

Once home, I took a deep breath and walked in the door. Ingrid and John sat at the dining room table, deep in discussion, a textbook open before them, and Mulder and Scully at their feet. They both laughed.

"Hi, honey," Ingrid said, and looked up. "How was your day?"

I can't explain what happened next. And I didn't want to think about what it meant. I just said it.

"Uneventful," I said, and walked over. "What are you guys reading?"

Was I a freak, too?

STATE HOSPITAL JOBS, caring for the chronically insane and now the criminally insane, usually in remote rural settings, have never been attractive to American-trained physicians. Beginning with Freudian psychoanalysis and its alluring emphasis on sex and unconscious drives, through the heady days of deinstitutionalization and the concomitant proliferation of psychological theories about mental illness—when it appeared that psychiatry might actually be at the vanguard of social change—dreary state hospitals and their relentlessly sick patients paled in comparison. Like the general public, three generations of American psychoanalysts, psychotherapists, and psychiatrists forgot state hospitals even existed.

In the mideighties, when the biologic revolution took hold, when mental illness was firmly tagged as structural and genetic in origin—like all other medical diseases—and when truly effective treatments finally became available, it was too late. Caring for the mentally sickest of our sick had already been outsourced to international doctors. And it remains that way still. Most state hospital psychiatrists, Napa State included, come from geographically diverse backgrounds.

This point was driven home one morning in mid-September when Monabong mentioned after rounds that the all-star squad from the patients' regular summer softball league had challenged the medical staff to a season-ending game.

"The Nuts versus the Quacks," Cohen said. "I like it."

As did I.

So after work that next Monday, I reported to the softball field for the medical staff's one Quack practice session.

Twelve physicians were in attendance. Most wore suit pants and hard shoes; some chatted amiably in Hindi, Urdu, or Arabic, others in English with clipped Indian accents. They, save Cohen, shared one thing in common: no one knew anything about softball.

Fielding gloves were routinely placed on the wrong hand. One person stepped up for batting practice and stood on home plate.

Another clutched the bat in the middle. With the finesse of eight-year-old girls, the doctors retrieved batted balls and awkwardly flung them toward the nearest base. Glasses fell off faces. Trousers split. Two fat lips resulted from thrown balls not being caught. It was mayhem, except for Cohen.

"My brothers and I played a little ball," Cohen said after he'd taken his turn at the plate and stroked pitch after pitch over a line of trees that formed the left-field fence.

I took my cuts as well. I'd played sports in high school. I could hold up my end, but that was about it.

The next afternoon, I watched the patients' practice. Somewhere between insanity and prison, they'd acquired an aptitude for softball. Boudreaux looked especially sharp. He and two men from Unit D lit up the fences. The Quacks were, it became readily apparent, going to get their clocks cleaned.

Game day dawned warm and still, one of those September afternoons for which baseball had been invented. The sun angled gently off a cloud as Cohen and I ambled from Unit C to the ball fields a few buildings over.

Cleats and gloves in hand, we made light chatter. We reached the pane of emerald grass that continued the ball field, sat on the curb, and changed our shoes.

As we did, a hospital van pulled up and out spilled the Nuts. Lingering grudges apparently forgotten for the day, the twelve men joshed, poked, and kidded. Boudreaux passed and tipped his cap. "Lovely day for a ball game, gentlemen," he said. "Let's play two."

"He's so odd," Cohen said. "Didn't he corner you once and threaten to kill you?"

"You heard about that?" I asked.

"Palanqui asked everyone to keep an eye on you," Cohen said.

"I needed it," I said, remembering back. "Still do."

Three staff members, NPR-man, and a trio of hospital cops got out of the van last, and then it pulled away.

"Next is *Fresh Air* with Terry Gross," NPR-man chirped. "Then news and traffic."

Cohen and I arrived in front of our bench, which ran parallel to the third-base line; the Nuts' bench mirrored it on the first base side. We played catch as the other doctors trickled in.

Despite a handout I'd distributed detailing the rules of baseball and tips for proper attire, the Quacks arrived, one after the other, still dressed in dark suit pants and button-down shirts. But they'd gotten two things right. Looking like a Nike ad, my squad wore spanking-new white baseball cleats. And they put their gloves on the correct hand.

All hospital units had permission to attend the game, and the small bleachers on either side of the field were packed with blue. An equal number of people trailed down both foul lines. I spotted McCoy, Caruthers, Mathews, Hong, and Cervantes, wearing new pink ear flags for the occasion, and most of the Unit C crew sitting on our side.

Staff persons were interspersed with the patients. I counted ten cops. The umpire was Sam Tillson, one half of our crack janitorial crew. He walked up carrying a canvas bag full of bats and balls, which he dumped out and distributed.

I met Tillson and a rangy member of the Nuts at home plate. "Doc, you'll be home team this year," Tillson said. "Mr. Wilson," he added to my blue-clad opponent, "your side will bat first." Wilson and I shook hands, then returned to our squads.

"We're home team so we hit last," I said, then called out our batting order and gave each person their positions on the field. "Okay, let's go," I enthused, and Cohen and I trotted away.

The rest of the Quacks meandered to the general vicinity of their assigned positions. Our center fielder stood five feet behind second base. I waved him backward, and as he jogged in the outfield grass, his shoes looked like white dice tumbling on a green felt casino table. I took my spot at shortstop. At first base, Cohen smiled behind the glove in front of his face.

"Play ball," Tillson shouted, and we were under way.

Boudreaux, the first Nut batter, roped a line drive that skipped past our startled Pakistani left fielder, who turned and watched the ball bounce away. As a baby-blue blur circled the bases, someone in the stands yelled, "Run, Forrest, run." Then all the Nuts took up the chant. I waved my arm like a windmill. "Go get it!" I shouted. Our fielder pointed to his chest. "Me?" he asked.

"Yes," I yelled. "Go get the ball." The slight man, in gray flannel slacks and porcelain-white shoes, turned and jogged away. He stopped abruptly, however, when a large peacock clattered down from a nearby tree branch. The flustered avian eyed the white orb that lay nestled in the outfield grass, then glared at our fielder. He pecked the ball. Then he stood tall, spread his tail, and let loose a shrill scream.

After a short standoff, the bird tired of the confrontation, struck his colors, and idly strolled away. Our fielder stepped forward, picked up the ball, and, like I'd shown him, cocked it behind his ear and threw his arm forward. Unfortunately, the ball never left his ear. As his hand shot through, the sphere dropped behind him.

With Boudreaux long across home plate, our fielder walked the ball toward the infield and threw it to me underhanded. It rolled a few feet from my glove. The Nuts convulsed in laughter. "Good hustle," I said. Our left fielder politely nodded and smiled.

We had a few more of these procedural calamities, but fewer and fewer as the game wore on. Everyone held the bat properly but most still swung as if they had a neurological disorder. Surprisingly, each batter managed to tap the ball someplace in the field. Most of the balls were hit so weakly, in fact, that the Nuts' infielders struggled to run in quickly enough before our batters scurried to first base. The Nuts, of course, rapidly caught on and began to play their people in so near home plate that toward the end of the game they and the batters could have almost shaken hands.

And so it went. Cohen and I accounted for a few runs. I was on base twice when he launched towering home runs over the trees in left field. The crowd went wild.

The Nuts showed their basic nature a time or two as well. NPR-man stunningly scorched a ball between two outfielders, and before they could sort themselves out and convey the ball plate-ward, NPR-man had easily scurried home. He became so excited, however, that he started to circle the bases a second time. Cohen snatched the ball from our startled pitcher, jogged between second and third base, and tagged NPR-man going by. Everyone turned to Tillson.

Surrounded by scores of excited psychopaths versus a dozen nattily clad international doctors, Tillson made the right call. "Safe," he cried, and the crowd erupted in cheers.

One call had been legitimately in dispute and went our way: A shot was slammed deep into the outfield, and our center fielder actually ran down the ball and threw a strike to Cohen, who whirled and whipped the ball to me as I covered home. I tagged the runner flying past and Tillson correctly called, "Out."

The runner, Mr. Spenser from Unit B, a large man apparently accustomed to getting his way, erupted in a fit. He berated poor Tillson and had to be physically restrained. In his agitated state, Spenser grabbed a bat off the ground but was quickly bundled away by his teammates.

I glanced at Cohen, who flicked his eyebrows. For a split second we both wondered how giving baseball bats to psychopaths had ever sounded like a good idea. Then we returned to our positions.

The game ended on time. The score was probably a hundred to five, but everyone had a good afternoon. The peacocks proved to be little further trouble, although a dozen or so had passed through the outfield during the fifth inning, delaying the game.

As we waited for the birds to clear the field, I turned to the line of seated Gomorrah doctors on our bench. "Where did those peacocks come from anyway?" I asked.

There was some general chatter. "We have no idea," one of the doctors replied. "They've always been here."

The last batter of the game, Spenser, the man who'd berated Tillson, shot a liner to the outfield again. Our fielder ran the ball down and heaved it to Cohen, who wisely held it. Spenser crossed home plate unhindered but scuffed by Tillson, who'd positioned himself to make another close call.

"Time's up," Tillson said, and looked at his watch.

The Quacks ran off the field, the Nuts celebrated, and we all shook hands. Turning, I saw Tillson walk away unsteadily. Twenty paces from the backstop, he collapsed face forward in the grass.

CHAPTER TWELVE

My insides contract–bad. "Who are you?" I ask right out loud. And he says what I've been afraid of since I killed Lester's father. "Haven't you guessed? I'm you. The real you."

–Bonnie Shimko, *You Know What You Have to Do*

Someone shouted and pointed at Tillson, and pandemonium erupted. A mass of blue surged toward the fallen man, interspersed with what was shown to be a startling lack of staff and security.

"Give him air!"

"Move back."

"Move up."

"Fuck you."

I picked my way through the mob and knelt beside Tillson, who lay in the grass, moaning and twisting as both hands grasped awkwardly for a prescription bottle that had rolled just out of reach. I snatched it up: nitroglycerin.

"He's having a heart attack," I said.

Caruthers and McCoy completed the inner circle around Tillson, who'd grown pallid. His breathing was shallow; the groaning had faded.

"Call 911," I shouted.

"Done," someone replied from somewhere in the crowd.

"I need room," I barked, my voice lost in the rising chorus of increasingly anxious gibbering that surrounded us. The crowd edged closer. The ring around Tillson began to close. And in it, five feet behind me, I saw Cervantes.

About to be swallowed by an avalanche of baby-blue humanity, I stood. Already I couldn't extend my arms. "Move back!" I yelled, and raised my hands above my head, gesturing as best I could. "Give us room!" But nothing happened. Elbows and shoulders constricted in from all sides.

I looked at Caruthers and McCoy.

"Goddamn it!" McCoy boomed, as he and Caruthers rose to their full height. "The man said move back!"

"Back!" Caruthers echoed.

And like the Red Sea before Moses, the crowd stepped away.

"Thank you," I said.

"You're welcome," McCoy and Caruthers replied in unison as I quickly scanned the sea of faces. Cervantes was gone.

On the ground, Tillson mumbled incoherently. I turned back around, swallowed my angst, and knelt, as did McCoy. Caruthers maintained crowd control.

I loosened Tillson's shirt.

"Are you okay?" McCoy said, and shook Tillson's shoulder.

Then Tillson stopped breathing.

"We need to do CPR," I said, and rolled Tillson onto his back.

"I'm CPR certified," McCoy said. "I'll do compressions."

Before I could reply, McCoy slid around to Tillson's side and placed the palm of one hand over Tillson's sternum and, both arms stiff, slid the other hand on top of the first. "Ready," he said.

"Okay," I said hesitantly.

McCoy rhythmically pumped Tillson's chest with exact force and metronomic precision. After a minute, he stopped. I checked for breathing or a heartbeat but got neither.

"Again," I said, and McCoy repeated the compression sequence. At the next rest interval, Tillson took a breath. I felt a pulse in his neck. His face began to pink. Thankfully, I heard the wail of a distant ambulance.

"He's coming around," I said.

McCoy leaned back and smiled.

As the siren grew louder, Cohen broke through the inner crowd wall. Standing next to Caruthers, he glanced at McCoy, the word *HELL* on his forehead glistening with sweat.

Then Cohen looked at me. "You all right?" he asked warily.

"I'm fine," I said.

"Make a path for the ambulance crew," Cohen shouted. The siren grew louder, then clipped off. No one moved.

McCoy stood. "Make way for the ambulance people," he thundered, and spread his arms. Once more the crowd separated. Two paramedics approached.

The medics assessed Tillson, began an IV, and hoisted him onto a stretcher. The crowd watched in silence as the medics loaded Tillson into the back of the ambulance and whisked him away. The show over, the patients gradually re-formed into unit-based groups and, led by what staff there were, slowly began to wander back to their various buildings.

McCoy and Caruthers joined the rest of the Unit C line. "Thanks again. Good job," I said.

"No problem," Caruthers replied.

"It was the least we could do," McCoy added, clearly pleased.

The Unit C group stepped away, but Cohen and I stayed back.

As we watched the patients shuffle off, I caught the glint of something metal on the ground. Unnoticed, I bent and plucked a sharpened eyeglass stem from the grass two feet behind me. With a chill, I slid it into the back pocket of my pants.

One of the Quacks walked up with Tillson's canvas equipment bag in hand. "What should I do with these?" he asked, and pulled out a bat the size of a bludgeon. "They got left on the field."

"I'll take everything back," Cohen said, and took the sack. "You know," he said, and looked into the sack of metal bats. "If those guys had been organized, they could have killed us all."

The next morning at rounds, before we discussed any patients, I pulled out the eyeglass stem from my pocket, removed a paper covering I'd applied, and set it on the conference table.

"I found this two feet behind me in the grass after the softball game," I said. "Cervantes threatened to stab me with one just like it the day of the shakedown."

Palanqui picked it up, examined it closely, and gently tapped the sharpened point on the table.

"What did he say to you?" Cohen said.

"He said he'd stab me if I didn't get him out of here."

"That's terrible," Monabong added.

"I'll call hospital police right now," Kate Henry said, and left the room.

"That little punk," Palanqui said.

"That little asshole," Cohen added.

"The team will talk to Cervantes after rounds, please," Xiang said.

An hour later, we found Cervantes in the day hall and asked him to accompany us back to his room.

"Dr. Seager said he found this in the grass after the softball game," Xiang said, and held out the shank in his open hand. The staff formed a crescent around Cervantes, who stood in the center of the room.

"I've never seen it before," Cervantes said. In addition to the usual paper mask and pink ear cloths, he sported brand-new horn-rimmed glasses.

"It's the same as the one we took off your bed during the shakedown," Cohen said sharply. "Dr. Seager said you threatened him with it."

"He's lying," Cervantes spat.

"Take Mr. Cervantes to the dayroom, please," Xiang said, and Monabong led him away. "We'll search the room."

"Cervantes has new glasses," Cohen said after the room search turned up nothing.

"I saw," I said.

FRIDAY MORNING, COHEN and I walked down the hallway to our offices; his was three doors down from mine. We stopped at the smell.

"Jesus," Cohen said, and looked around. "Who died?"

I saw Hancock headed our way. She walked up and made a face. "It's back," she said.

"You've had this smell before?" I asked. I'd once left a fish in a tackle box for a month. It smelled like that.

"It's come and gone over the years," she said.

"What is it?" Cohen asked.

"Nobody knows," Hancock replied.

RETURNING FROM LUNCH, Cohen and I entered the main unit building, passing cops who were heading out. As we exchanged greetings, an alarm rang and everyone took off at full speed.

I unlocked the unit door, let the others fly past, then locked the door and joined the rush.

"Room twelve," Kate Henry shouted as we ran by the nurses' station toward Smith's room. I stopped in the doorway.

On the floor, Xiang wrestled with Smith, dice rumbling at their feet. His two roommates, the other legs of the gambling tripod, tried to kick Xiang, but Cohen quickly herded them out the door.

Cole rushed into the room and ripped Smith off Xiang. "Leave me alone, you son of a bitch!" Smith shouted, and continued to thrash, but Cole managed to get him into the hallway. A group of patients watched from the end of the corridor. As Cole maneuvered toward the restraint room, Smith wiggled his left arm free and smacked his fist into Cole's jaw.

"You fucking idiot!" Cole boomed, and grabbed two huge handfuls of Smith's shirt, lifting him off the ground.

"You're breaking my arm, you fucking Nazi," Smith shouted, and summoned one final surge of energy, nearly spinning free. But Cole, red-faced, biceps bulging, snagged Smith by both shoulders and slammed him against the hallway wall with his massive body. Smith screamed.

This brought shouts of protest from the clustered patients.

Cole turned his head. “Do you gentlemen have a problem?” he spat. The patients fell quiet.

Xiang appeared, syringe in hand. The cops quickly pushed Smith into the restraint room, and Xiang followed. I looked back at the patients.

“That kind of stuff okay with you, Doc?” McCoy called down the corridor. He fixed me in a glare and a rattle went up my spine.

“No,” I called back. “But you can’t hit a cop, either.”

McCoy continued to stare.

I joined Xiang and the cops on their way back to the nurses’ station.

“Show’s over, gentlemen,” Xiang said to the various patients. “To the courtyard or your rooms, please.”

Cohen and I stood in the nurses’ station and watched the patients pass by. Jaws firm, no one looked inside. Nor did they look at the cops who stood against the far hallway wall straightening their shirts and checking equipment belts. This done, the cops headed to the exit. Cole turned while going out the door.

“Another day in paradise,” he said.

FOR THE REMAINDER of that day and most of the next the patients were unsettled, their tempers short. The staff was disquieted and edgy. The incident between Cole and Smith reminded everyone just how close to the surface chaos truly lived; how near to detonation we’d come. We knew that one careless word or thoughtless action would have set off the powder keg.

Driving home, I thought about a lot of things. Smith and Cole. McCoy and Wilkins. Gomez and Palanqui. Mathews, Luella, and

Dr. Tom. And I came back to what Larsen had said. When you're continually surrounded by violence and fear, you begin to see things differently. You know danger is omnipresent but you pretend it's not. You pretend that, all evidence to the contrary, things are okay.

I realized that the sickness at Gomorrah was violence but the symptom was denial. Wilkins, Luella, and Dr. Tom were rarely spoken about. And if they were, the subject was quickly changed. They made things too real. So we ignored them. We acted like nothing had happened. We went about our business.

On Monday morning, a week after the softball game, as we gathered in the nurses' station before rounds, I realized I'd finally begun to feel like a part of Gomorrah. I liked the staff with whom I worked. To a person, they seemed professional and competent. I'd gotten to know my patients and liked most of them. We hadn't had a major blowup in a while. Things, I concluded, were going pretty well. That morning I felt something new since coming to Gomorrah—confidence.

Cohen and I walked into the nurses' station, where the staff was gathered. Xiang was on the phone, his shoulders slumped. He spoke softly, hung up the receiver, and turned. "Dr. Tom died last night," Xiang said, and for the next few minutes the only sound in the station was a faint clock ticking.

"I met Dr. Tom ten years ago," Kate Henry said finally. "On my first day here. I was young and nervous. He went out of his way to make things easier for me. It was a kindness I've never forgotten."

Palanqui spoke up. "Do you remember the day Dr. Tom came to work wearing those big red clown shoes?"

"For the Halloween party on Friday," Hancock said, and broke out in a grin.

"Only he got confused and wore the shoes on Thursday instead," Randy said.

The staff shared more stories, shed a few tears, and laughed together.

"I know the patients have feelings for Dr. Tom, too," Monabong said, and we agreed that a memorial gathering for them would follow that afternoon.

"What about Mr. Mathews?" Palanqui asked.

"I don't know . . ." Kate Henry said.

"He's a murderer now," I added.

"They're all murderers," Cohen countered, and that brought the discussion to a close.

That afternoon in the off-unit community room, the fifty chairs we'd set up filled fast. Mathews attended the servicc and sat between Carver and McCoy.

Some of the older residents spoke haltingly. "I liked Dr. Tom," Ortega said, and everyone agreed. A few got off track, but Cohen steered them back.

"It's the doing of communists," an older man sneered.

"Even the communists are sad today," Cohen said calmly.

"Who's Dr. Tom?" another elderly patient asked. He suffered from dementia.

"Dr. Tom was a friend to everyone on Unit C," Cohen replied.

Boudreaux spoke of Yale University, from which both he and Dr. Tom had matriculated. "Dr. Tom, may I find you on the campus green. May we walk the halls of the Sterling Library. May we listen to the Whiffenpoofs. Fight on, fellow Eli, and farewell."

Near the end of the service, Mathews looked as if he wanted to speak and began to rise. I held my breath, but McCoy placed a hand firmly on his knee. Instead Caruthers stood and summed up the consensus. "Dr. Tom, we loved you and we miss you," he said, and glanced up. "Godspeed, my friend."

The rest of the week a dreary fog hung over Unit C. Flowers and sympathy cards adorned the nurses' station. Hancock and I volunteered to stay behind and cover the unit while the remaining staff attended the Friday funeral. That afternoon, McCoy stopped me in the hallway.

"You're not going to Dr. Tom's services?" he asked.

"I didn't know Dr. Tom," I said.

"He was a nice man."

"That's what I hear."

McCoy scanned up and down the hallway. "Somebody should blow this place up," he said, and walked away.

THE NEXT MORNING, both patients and staff got back to routine. At least on the outside. The staff was hurting. They had the awful conundrum of knowing that Dr. Tom had been murdered by a person they dealt with every day. A person who would never be called to account for his crimes. And who could murder again.

I realized as well that the patients faced this same dilemma. They had to live with Mathews, too. But it got complicated after that. Hadn't many of them murdered also? Maybe it wasn't that Mathews had murdered per se, but that he'd murdered so recently. And he killed someone we all knew, in our home.

For the staff, as all medical people learn to do, the raw feelings gradually got sealed up and swallowed. We had care to deliver. Medications to pass. Therapy to administer. We had a job to do. People depended on us. We had to move on. So we did. And remembering the past wasn't part of that paradigm. Although Dr. Tom's name would be mentioned occasionally over the ensuing months, it was with a sense of sad resignation more than anything else.

INGRID AND I sat alone after dinner. She took a breath. "It's time to talk about your job again."

"It's past time," I said.

"You haven't mentioned it much lately."

"No, I haven't."

Ingrid paused. "Does that mean things have settled down?"

"It's getting better, I think," I ventured, and Ingrid smiled.

"I spoke with the Realtor in Utah today," she said. "We have an offer on our house."

"A short sale?"

"No. A real offer." Ingrid beamed. "The nightmare is finally over."

"That's great," I said.

"We'll clear enough money to make a down payment on a home here," Ingrid went on. "But since we're both new to our jobs, we'll need two incomes to qualify for a mortgage. And I'm not going to lock us into anything if your job . . . or you get . . . You know what I mean."

"We shouldn't sign a mortgage," I countered, "if Mr. McCoy is going to kill me?"

"That's pretty much it," Ingrid said.

I had only a split second. "I think I'm going to be okay," I said. "I can't guarantee anything. But I think so. I'm getting to know some of the patients pretty well, and the place doesn't feel as tense. And I'm less worried about Mr. McCoy."

"You plan to stay at Gomorrah, then?"

I was in deep. "Yes. I think things will be fine."

"What changed?" she asked.

"I did, or the patients did," I said. "I don't know, something did."

Ingrid looked me in the eye. "Then I can find a Realtor here?" she asked.

The words just came out. "By all means."

Ingrid's eyes didn't waver. "Are you telling me that those psychopaths are somehow different now?"

"We seem to be getting along better."

"And you trust this change?"

"I do," I said.

So I stayed. Though I thought I knew why, I didn't really understand my decision until I spoke with Dr. Cohen the next day.

We sat again at the metal picnic table just outside the fence and pulled Mexican food from paper bags.

"Do you remember that carton-of-cigarettes thing?" Cohen said, and unwrapped a taco. "Did you ever find out who those people were?"

"Detective Levin from hospital police hinted I might have done it," I said. "Because I reported it."

"You gotta love this place," Cohen said with a laugh.

"You still plan on staying, then?" I asked.

"Of course," Cohen said. "Where else would I go?" Then he looked at me. "You still thinking about leaving?"

I set down my food. "I was until I spoke with Ingrid last night. We finally sold our house in Utah. She says we can swing a mortgage here if we have two incomes. She loves her job. She's really happy."

"You're staying, then?"

"I am."

"That's awesome," Cohen said, and took another bite of food. Then he looked at me and laughed. "It's perfect," he added. "You get to stay here, which is what you really wanted all along, but you can blame your wife if things don't work out."

"What are you talking about?" I asked, stumbling over the words.

"Nice work," Cohen said, and patted me on the arm. "Very devious. I'm proud of you."

"That's not what I—"

"And it sounds like your wife bought it," Cohen went on. "I underestimated you." Cohen looked at his watch. "I'd better be careful," he said. "Next you'll convince me I was one of those people selling cigarettes behind the unit."

I was too taken aback to reply.

Cohen stood. "I'm late for the Psychology Department meeting," he said, then balled up his paper bag and strode away.

CHAPTER THIRTEEN

When dealing with the insane, the best method is to pretend to be sane.

—Hermann Hesse

Summer slowly became fall. In Northern California, autumn brings no New England bite. Frost is rare, but leaves turn. Green bleeds into yellow and vivid red, setting vineyards ablaze.

"We're hosting the annual Halloween party this Friday," Palanqui said after rounds on a Monday in late October.

"A party for the staff?" I asked.

"It's an event for the patients," Monabong said.

"Do they trick-or-treat from unit to unit?" Cohen asked, smiling.

"Now that would be interesting," Palanqui said.

"Every year the hospital sponsors a dance," Xiang said. "This time we are the host unit. We provide music and decorations. It's a big deal. The guys get slicked up. Ladies' ward attends, too."

"And they actually dance?" I asked.

"This I gotta see," Cohen added.

"We need chaperones," Palanqui said. "Can we count you two in?"

"Of course," I said.

"Maybe Dr. Seager and I will bust some moves," Cohen said.

"I'd buy a ticket for that," Palanqui concluded.

On Wednesday morning, I went through the sally port as usual, but the middle gate didn't buzz. Instead, an officer rapped on the thick glass. I tensed. A small panel slid open and, like the scene at the castle in *The Wizard of Oz*, a face appeared in the small window. "You Dr. Seager?" the man asked.

"Yes," I replied nervously.

The face disappeared and a hand shot out holding a single sheet of paper. "For you," the man said.

I took the paper and read it quickly. It was a subpoena from the San Francisco County Superior Court, "commanding" my presence to testify as a witness in a jury trial concerning the possible release of William James McCoy. It was scheduled for mid-December.

Oh, Lord, I thought. Testifying against a patient is the single most dangerous thing a psychiatrist can do. From the witness stand you explain how sick and dangerous a person remains while they're sitting in the courtroom with you. Patients always take it personally. Many plot revenge.

After rounds that morning, as we filed down the hallway, the unit door opened and in stepped a woman, late twenties, blond hair, clear blue eyes. She locked the door behind her and turned. Cohen and I shared a confused glance.

"Emily Carstairs," Xiang said. "New social work intern. I met her yesterday. She's assigned with Ms. Larsen for three months."

Carstairs walked down the corridor and every patient stopped short. Like a hound on a scent, McCoy skidded out of his room, pushed back his hair, and quickly strode to Carstairs's side. The other patients backed away. Carstairs appeared unnerved, but McCoy remained the gentleman.

"I'm sorry to frighten you," he said, and took a step back and extended his hand. "My name is William McCoy."

Xiang dashed up and intercepted Carstairs before she could return the handshake and led her to the nurses' station.

"Mr. Xiang, you're killing my action," McCoy said with pseudo-indignation. Carstairs glanced back. McCoy shone.

In the nurses' station, Xiang and Carstairs faced the staff. Carstairs introduced herself and shook each hand in turn as we gave our names. "It's a pleasure to meet you all," she said, and any previous discomfort dissipated.

"Very glad to have you here," Xiang said.

"Stay away from Mr. McCoy," Cohen added.

"What?" Carstairs asked.

"The man in the hallway with *HELL* tattooed on his forehead," Cohen replied. "Makes him easy to spot."

"Best avoid him," Xiang concluded.

Larsen approached Carstairs. "Let's go back to my office," she said, and the pair headed off.

I glanced down the hallway and caught sight of McCoy, his gaze still locked on Carstairs.

Fortunately, Carstairs was on a Monday-Wednesday-Friday schedule. Unit C couldn't have handled having her around more often. As it was, it took the staff a concerted effort to keep McCoy from bursting at the seams. On each appointed day, he met Carstairs at the door, escorted her to the nurses' station through a suddenly empty hallway, then gallantly retired to his room. We tried getting to the door before him, but McCoy had some sort of radar. When

Carstairs's key hit the lock, he appeared. After a while, it became part of the unit routine. And Carstairs didn't seem anxious anymore.

On the day of the Halloween dance, Cohen and I helped escort the Unit C contingent from our building to the main recreation hall across campus. In an excited state, the men overflowed with bravado: they joked, pushed shoulders, and laughed out loud.

The sight of the women patients, hair combed, clad in clean, ironed blue scrubs, however, brought the jocularity and horseplay to an end. The Unit C men straightened shirts and smoothed unruly hair. One man rubbed the toes of his tennis shoes on the backs of his pant legs.

Walking into the recreation hall, a basketball court with the baskets pulled up, the Unit C people behaved in an orderly and surprisingly calm fashion. Other units arrived, until the rec hall walls were lined with blue uniforms. Kate Henry made some introductory remarks, music started, and the festivities began.

Things got off to a slow start. A few folks danced, but many patients seemed uncertain what to do. A large contingent of men, mainly the older set, stood in a line as if petrified. Others, like Cervantes, Hong, and the wheelchair-bound, simply waited courtside and watched nervously.

Not unexpectedly, once things got going, Caruthers, McCoy, Boudreaux, and the higher-functioning men from other units stole the show. They danced with all the willing women and kept the gathering lively.

The music, emanating from a CD player and speakers balanced on folding chairs, was an eclectic mix ranging from fifties doo-wop and the Beatles to Nirvana and hip-hop. The plan was to play at least one song with which each person could identify.

Scattered at random around the hall were men who were unclear, it seemed, on the concept of dancing. But they loved the music. NPR-man among them, they convulsed, flung, and kicked in a whirligig patchwork. In tribute to the evening, NPR-man managed to pace his verbal output in eerie sync with the music. It was vaguely hypnotic: NPR rap set to the tune of "Proud Mary."

NPR-man stood in the center of the basketball court and shouted, "I'm Ira Glass, from *This American Life*. My producer is Doug Berman. He's no slave to fashion. Not Hillary Clinton. He's no woman." The crowd cheered.

Behind this mélange of activity stood a punch bowl and rows of paper cups. A dozen carved pumpkins lined the dais.

Unlike at a regular dance, however, there was a strong police presence. Keeping a stoic mien, two dozen hospital cops lined either side of the gym. They got called into action only once, when, in response to a commotion in the far corner, they discovered a couple in flagrante delicto.

Gomorrah is a coed institution. While men outnumber women almost nine-to-one, women-only and mixed units exist. During orientation, the Patient Rights Department stated clearly that sexual relations were a normal part of life and could not be curtailed as long as those relations were consensual, not abusive, and "didn't interfere with either person's treatment plan." There had been, we were told, weddings and babies born at Gomorrah.

Thankfully, no fights erupted. No one got punched or stabbed. The soiree lasted an hour and a half and was considered a success.

Some of the patients and most of the Unit C staff stayed behind to clean up. We folded and put away chairs, took down streamers, and removed wall decorations. Lastly, we began to stow the carved pumpkins. Some of the men seemed drawn to them; they stood quietly and stared. Cohen and I both noticed.

"How was Halloween when you were a kid?" Cohen asked Caruthers.

Caruthers laughed. "In Watts?" he said. "Dr. Seager, you been there. Can you imagine a kid dressed in a clown suit going door-to-door?"

I shook my head.

"He'd last a minute," Boudreaux drawled.

"If that long," an older man said, and angled in his wheelchair.

"I hear that," a second senior citizen chirped, and everyone laughed.

"How about you?" Caruthers asked Cohen.

"Are you kidding?" Cohen said. "Halloween was the biggest night of the year. My friends and I mapped out the neighborhood like a military maneuver."

"It must have been great," Caruthers said. "All that candy. And the costumes."

"No bullets," Boudreaux said.

"My sister and I went as Donny and Marie Osmond one year," I said.

"My brothers and I were the Marx Brothers," Cohen added, and tapped the ash from an imaginary cigar.

McCoy hefted two pumpkins, turned, and set them down on a trolley beside him. "Our next-door neighbor in Stockton killed his wife one Halloween," McCoy said, and turned back. "Blew her head off with a shotgun. Both barrels. A friend and I were standing outside on the sidewalk. We were Luke Skywalker and Han Solo. Lead, blood, and glop came flying through that door. What a mess."

Again, the wrenching incongruity of Gomorrah struck me in the face. What do you say to a murderer who tells you a dreadful Halloween story from his childhood? How are you supposed to feel? I didn't like thinking that some of the men even had childhoods. Hadn't some of them stolen those same childhoods from their victims? Where do you learn to balance such things?

We stood in silence as McCoy continued to load pumpkins. "You guys paralyzed?" he asked, and flung two more large pumpkins up onto the trolley. I looked at Cohen. He raised his eyebrows. We each grabbed a pumpkin and joined him.

CHAPTER FOURTEEN

In their brief time together Slothrop forms the impression that this octopus is not in good mental health, though where's his basis for comparing?

—Thomas Pynchon, *Gravity's Rainbow*

Fall swung toward winter. By mid-November we'd had a stretch of quiet on Unit C. Maybe it was the dance, the pumpkins, who knew? But for two weeks no fists were thrown, no wheelchairs rammed, no alarms pulled. The calm wouldn't last, but it was nice to see how things could be.

I took this opportunity to do something I'd meant to do for a long time. I checked out the staff's therapy groups.

"Gentlemen, we have Anger Management Group in the day hall," Larsen announced over the intercom one morning after rounds. "Everyone's invited."

Twenty-four people filed into the assigned room. I watched from just outside the door and was taken aback. Whatever danger I confronted on Unit C paled in comparison to that faced by the therapists. At the back of the dayroom, Larsen stood, marker in hand, before a whiteboard. Two dozen criminally insane men sat between her and the door.

I scouted the patients. Some paid attention. Some slept. Others mumbled. Mathews stared out the window. McCoy clandestinely sold a cigarette to Carver. NPR-man jabbered. In the far corner, Gomez was masturbating.

I looked at other groups over the week. In a studio just off the outside hallway, Craft Class seemed somewhat better. At least the men had something to occupy their hands. Monabong, alone among them, walked from table to table.

Finally I checked in on Cohen as he conducted Life Skills Class. Standing at the front of the day hall, I couldn't hear what he said, but he had everyone's attention. He opened his arms wide, bent his knees, and jumped on top of a table. Laughter rolled out the door.

If Cohen got in trouble, at least he could always leap out of the room.

At the end of the week I wished I hadn't seen the therapy groups. I knew they were valuable and the patients said they enjoyed them. But I couldn't rid from my mind the image of Larsen standing before a score of psychotic men, one with an erect penis in his hand.

"We need help with the Thanksgiving luncheon," Hancock said on Wednesday after rounds, as we sat around the cramped conference room table.

"Luncheon?" I asked.

"It's a meal for the patients and their families," Hancock said.

I was planning on a nice holiday dinner with my in-laws. I hadn't realized the hospital would formally celebrate it, too.

"It's great to see so many families reunited," Kate Henry added. "If only for a couple of hours, especially for the men with children."

Cohen tilted his head. "This lunch is for all the patients?"

"Every patient on every unit," Xiang said.

"And kids are invited?"

"We strongly encourage our men to stay connected to their children," Kate Henry said.

Cohen and I thought the same thing. "What about the sexual predators?" he asked.

"We keep a close eye on things," Kate Henry concluded in a tone that said the subject was closed. There was a beat of silence.

"Can we count on you guys?" Palanqui asked brightly.

"Of course," I said.

"Wouldn't miss it," Cohen added.

I stopped Cohen in the hall that afternoon. "Are they serious about this family lunch thing?" I asked.

"Seems so."

"Let me get this straight," I said. "The hospital is going to invite a bunch of children to have lunch in a room into which they've also invited the state's most notorious child molesters?"

"Not to worry," Cohen said. "They're going to keep an eye on things."

The next day, my in-laws arrived for Thanksgiving. They kissed John on each cheek, then held him at arm's length. "He's getting so tall," my mother-in-law said. "And so handsome." She ruffled John's hair and beamed. "Takes after his grandmother," she added.

Ingrid's parents were John's only connection to their generation. In 1941, both had been near John's age when the Germans invaded Denmark. Trapped, my future in-laws spent their teen years under the brutal Nazi boot. They met during that terrible period and married after the war and had stories but rarely chose to tell them. They appreciated life in America in a way I would never truly understand.

This situation was something that John seemed to intuit. He understood he was living and sharing with his grandparents the years stolen from them by the war. It was apparent in the way he and they shared a casual glance or tiny smile. They could sit without talking and know what the others were thinking. My in-laws' unbridled enthusiasm for the minutiae of John's life displayed unfettered love and deep connection. Ingrid and I had both noticed it.

Leaving for work the next morning, I stopped in the doorway. On the coffee table in front of the living room couch lay two huge empty popcorn bowls and a dozen drained soda cans. The air still hung with the smell of kringle—a special marzipan pastry ordered from a Danish bakery in Solvang—and the faint echo of laughter that had filled the room the night before. I smiled and headed to my car.

When I got to Unit C, rounds were short. "Big day," Kate Henry said as the staff gathered in the conference room. "Thanksgiving lunch. We've got a million things to do."

"We'll need you guys at ten thirty," Palanqui said.

"No problem," I replied.

"We're there," Cohen chimed in.

At ten fifteen, we headed toward the same rec hall that had held the Halloween dance. To our left, the sally port bulged with people. Hospital cops wanded and searched as fast as possible. A line snaked back through the parking lot. Children ran everywhere.

Rows of standard cafeteria tables and plastic chairs, the kind anyone would recognize from their school days, filled the rec hall.

Two big bays, opening into kitchens on either side of the room, billowed steam as workers removed turkeys from industrial ovens.

Tables soon filled with bowls of green salad, candied yams, peas, biscuits, mashed potatoes, and pumpkin pies. As soon as Cohen and I headed in, Palanqui walked over. "Pick a spot," she said. "We need servers."

Cohen stood behind a tray of yams. I chose a big salver of peas. Then the front doors swung open, and, unit by unit, the patients arrived and took seats at preassigned tables, leaving spaces for family members. The last group in, the doors closed again. A dozen cops stood guard in front of the portals.

Even with all the patients seated, the room was oddly quiet. The staff conversed, but the patients said little. Most sat with hands folded atop the tables, nervously glancing at the doors. The anticipation was intensified by the entrance of a dozen turkeys from the kitchens, hot and golden brown, on wooden carving platters.

The doors finally opened again and family members streamed in, craning their necks and searching for the correct table. Hugs were exchanged, some awkward, some not. Children buzzed and pulled at their mothers' arms.

Once situated, the occupants of each table rose in turn, lined up, plates in hand, and the meal was served. Kate Henry, Dr. Francis, and a host of other administrators carved and apportioned out the turkeys.

I ladled peas with a grin and made small talk. Randy wheeled Burns through the line and paid him special attention, being certain that he got his food just the way he wanted. Caruthers came by with Ortega. "Happy holidays," I said.

"*Feliz día de Acción de Gracias,*" Ortega said in reply.

I spoke briefly with relatives of Hong and Cervantes. Alex Mathews came through with an attractive wife and two ten-year-old boys. "These are the twins," Mathews said.

"Fine-looking boys," I said. "You must be proud."

"We are," their mother said.

"Thanks, Doc," McCoy said at his turn. He was in line alone.

As was Boudreaux. "Not the kind of food you're accustomed to, I'll bet," I said when Boudreaux stepped up.

"Every year my grandmother makes a turducken," Boudreaux said.

I ladled peas onto his plate. "A what?"

"Turducken is a chicken cooked inside a duck inside a turkey," Boudreaux said. "Throw in some fresh oyster corn bread and crayfish stuffing and you've got something special."

"It sounds terrific," I said.

"But it's not the food I miss, Doc," Boudreaux continued. "It's my family. Ever since . . . well, you know. We haven't had much contact."

"Happy Thanksgiving, Mr. Boudreaux," I said.

"Same to you, Dr. Seager," Boudreaux replied, and moved on.

Like Boudreaux and McCoy, many patients didn't have family in attendance. A large number came, ate, and left. Others hadn't come at all. I didn't see NPR-man or Mr. Smith. I'd planned to sit and speak with each Unit C family, but the lines were long and everyone was hungry. The time just passed. And when it came down to it, that was weirdly okay.

Food served, Cohen and I had the chance to eat a bite and watch the remainder of the event unfold. It was good to see the patients who clearly enjoyed their family members. Occasionally laughter rang out. But in truth, they were the minority. The general feeling in the hall, and for me, was one of odd angst.

Many families ate quietly, barely looking at one another. They seemed to occupy the same space only by random chance. A parent would ask a question but receive no reply. Not even a glance. Another question would come a bit later. Silence.

Some parents carried on a monologue with their patient-children, reciting family news and neighborhood updates, but never getting anything in return.

A dozen patients ate alone and then sat alone. I looked at Cohen. We'd been joined by Hancock. "Some of them killed their family," Hancock pointed out.

"Villegas murdered his father," Cohen said. "But his mom still comes to see him."

"Of course," Hancock said. "She's his mother."

We were silent for a while. "If mental illness is genetic," I said, giving voice to something I'd noticed ever since coming to psychiatry, "why do the parents seem so normal?"

A gaggle of kids rambled by, whooping and chasing one another. No adults followed. At the other end of the room, Kate Henry was engrossed in conversation with Dr. Francis. I scanned the tables and caught McCoy's eye. He sat with Mathews and his wife. McCoy winked, and I got a chill.

"Does anyone else think this is the screwiest thing we've ever done?" I asked.

But Hancock had turned to speak with someone, and Cohen had wandered off.

• • •

AFTER KATE HENRY thanked everyone for coming and made some final remarks, she told the families to say their farewells. The goodbyes proved sad or strange or both. A few children cried. Then the police escorted our visitors out of the rec hall and off hospital grounds.

The patients formed into groups and walked back to their units. Cohen and I stayed behind to help clean up. While others washed and put away the dishes, we bussed the serving area, then folded and stacked tables.

As I was leaving the rec hall a short while later, I met Hancock in the doorway heading out. She stood and looked at the line of parents waiting to exit the sally port. "There but for the grace of God . . ." she said.

CHAPTER FIFTEEN

I happen to be partial to humans—most anyway. Clowns, not so much. Those evil bastards never stop smiling.

—Mimi Jean Pamfiloff, *Accidentally . . . Evil?*

Thanksgiving weekend was a joy. For four days, surrounded by family, we watched all of John's favorite movies, ate tons of great food, and talked about a million things, none of which involved murder, rape, or lunacy. I knew my in-laws were curious about my job. The conversation veered there only once.

"I imagine your work is interesting, Stephen?" my mother-in-law asked, and Ingrid quickly changed the subject. But later, as we stood side by side at the sink washing dishes, Ingrid brought it back up.

"How is your job?" she asked.

"It's all right."

A pause. "You're lying, aren't you?"

"Some," I said.

DURING THE TIME of Dickens, London's mentally ill were housed in Bethlehem Hospital, or "Bedlam," as it was pronounced in Cockney. On weekends, the upper crust of English society took family outings to the facility, where, for a fee, the most debilitated patients were put on display and openly mocked. Early American mental institutions copied this lucrative enterprise. The brain-diseased, it was believed, had lost the ability to reason—something highly prized during the Enlightenment period—and had thus become akin to wild animals and deserved the brutal abuse they received.

The treatment of brain disease during this time involved shocking the unfortunates back to reality. Therapies included whippings, beatings, bleeding, electrical jolts (usually to the genitals), starvation, total isolation, and chemical skin burns.

When not involved in "treatment," patients were chained to the wall by limb and neck restraints in the standing position. Leeway was granted enough to eat, but sleep was not accommodated. The brain-diseased lived in crusting, fetid rags above mounting piles of their own waste. Clothing wasn't changed, nor were the cells ever cleaned.

At the beginning of the nineteenth century, two persons, one a French physician, the other an English tea merchant, recognized this therapeutic model as flawed and proposed coincident plans for remediation. In 1792 Philippe Pinel, the French doctor, struck the chains from forty-nine sick men at the Bicêtre, a notoriously wretched Paris mental facility. In London, a crusading Quaker, William Tuke, the tea seller, founded the York Retreat in 1796, and introduced compassionate care.

Tuke and Pinel instituted reforms called "moral treatment," which emphasized a homelike atmosphere for care of the brain-diseased. Forbidding the use of restraints or punishment, the overarching principles for this new therapy became "sympathy and kindness."

In the United States, moral treatment was championed by a Massachusetts woman, Dorothea Lynde Dix. Owing to poor health, Ms. Dix traveled to England seeking medical care. During her stay, she was introduced to an array of English social reformers, including the followers of Tuke. Dix toured the York Retreat and was amazed.

During the last half of the nineteenth century, touting the moral treatment model she'd witnessed in England, Dix was instrumental in facilitating the construction of thirty-two American state hospitals for the insane. They were called "asylums"—places of refuge.

Enamored with the value of caring treatment, Dix claimed—with no supporting evidence—that these new asylums, in and of themselves, would lead to a cure for chronic mental illness.

Over the ensuing decades, however, any crusading zeal or therapeutic optimism was extinguished by two World Wars and the Great Depression. The brain-diseased in their remote asylums reassumed low national priority. Left to their own devices, the new mental hospitals filled to capacity. Budgets were cut. Renovation and upkeep stopped. Staff numbers dwindled. Care became banal and unfocused, sanitation eroded, food grew scarce.

And making matters worse, the brain-diseased didn't get well in the state asylums; they only got sicker. Hope was replaced by the grinding reality of chronic mental illness. It remained, as it always had been, a problem stubbornly resistant to therapeutic efforts. Care for the brain-diseased had morphed into what was rightly coined "warehousing."

After World War II, however, driven by published reports on the dreary conditions at state asylums—written by conscientious objectors assigned to the hospitals as an alternative to military duty—the grim atmosphere came to light in a series of exposés, culminating in the seminal work *The Shame of the States*. It was a ringing denunciation of the bleak American asylum system written in 1948 by Albert Deutsch. *Life* magazine ran distressing pictures. Over the following years, public opinion gradually remobilized. Reform of state mental institutions once again became a priority.

These efforts culminated in 1955 with formation of a federal Joint Commission on Mental Illness and Health (JCMH). The commission's charge was to sift through all currently available information on the cause and treatment of mental illness and to make specific recommendations that could be instituted nationwide. The commission's final report, *Action for Mental Health*, was released in 1961.

In 1963, spearheaded by President John Kennedy, whose sister Rosemary suffered from mental illness, the JCMH report led to the enactment of the Community Mental Health Act, which called for a thorough and revolutionary retooling of the entire US mental-health-care system. The locus of treatment would be transferred away from the dank state hospitals to a new coordinated network of Community Mental Health Centers.

These new community centers would, the report said, deliver prompt, intense, and inclusive "point of contact" treatment in local cities and towns, which would, they concluded—also without any evidence—prevent the development of chronic mental illness and obviate any further need for state hospitals.

For individual states, the financial benefits of this new arrangement were obvious. Funding dried up, and the state hospitals were emptied.

Three Supreme Court decisions made certain they weren't filled again. In *Lessard v. Schmidt* (1972), *O'Connor v. Donaldson* (1975), and *Suzuki v. Quisenberry* (1976), the Court clearly stated that a person could not be involuntarily hospitalized if they could "survive" in the community. These decisions named dangerousness the core issue, not need for treatment. And in *Donaldson*, the justices specifically affirmed an involuntarily hospitalized patient's right to full substantive legal due process.

The above measures were universally hailed as progress and seen as a major humanitarian step forward. The results, however, have proven otherwise.

The state hospitals emptied and their seriously mentally ill patients were sent back to receive care in the communities. Local communities, however, hadn't been consulted and they showed no interest whatever in a massive influx of psychotic individuals. Congress never adequately funded the Community Mental Health Centers, so most weren't built. The newly released state-hospital patients, with nowhere to live and no place to receive treatment, took up residence on city streets and became the homeless mentally ill.

Seventy percent of homeless mentally ill persons eventually run afoul of the law and spend time in jail, where they are housed without adequate treatment—warehoused. Upon release, the mentally ill persons return to the streets, eventually get rearrested, spend more time in jail, and then are released again, ad infinitum.

Now sitting empty and without funding, the state hospitals morphed into "forensic" facilities, specializing in the treatment of mentally ill criminals for whose care the states would still pay.

Thus, an unusual situation resulted. State-hospital patients became the urban homeless mentally ill and ended up in jail. Jails, geared for criminals, filled with mentally ill people. And the state hospitals, best suited to care for the mentally ill, instead housed criminals.

THAT NEXT WEEK, I used my lunch hours to pore over Bill McCoy's old hospital records and his Unit C chart. I needed to know the information cold. I took copious notes.

Cohen, sticking his head in the door, saw me buried in work. "Court tomorrow?"

"San Francisco," I said.

In our state, the county in which a crime occurs maintains jurisdiction over our committed patients. And all mental-health court business is transacted in that home county. We live in a large state. You can drive many hours to reach a remote locale. And a jury trial could last an entire day or more.

"It seems like a slam dunk," Cohen said. "If McCoy's not dangerous, who is?"

The past few days, I'd thought about McCoy's case a lot. And I had a real problem. Cohen was right—McCoy was the most dangerous person I'd ever known. But that wasn't the issue. Whether that dangerousness resulted from a mental illness was going to be the point. And that meant a current mental illness. Not back when he killed the gas station man. It meant a mental illness now.

Bill McCoy wasn't mentally ill. Probably never had been. He'd been high on methamphetamine when he committed his crimes. The records were clear about that. I knew it. McCoy knew it. And you can bet McCoy's defense attorney knew it. It was going to be messy.

"We'll see how things go," I said to Cohen.

I dropped some charts off in the nurses' station before I left that afternoon. McCoy bounded out of his room as I walked by.

"Big day tomorrow," he said.

"Mr. McCoy, I wish you the best," I said, and walked away.

I felt odd. I'd watched McCoy assault a man and probably kill him. But he was my patient. We'd performed CPR together and saved a life. We'd exchanged Halloween stories. I had a sworn ethical duty to put his welfare above mine. But I also had to testify against him and I knew he wouldn't like it. I was in over my head.

Robert Leung—Asian, early thirties, pleasant face, an assistant San Francisco County district attorney—stood as I walked into his office. "Dr. Seager?" he asked.

"Mr. Leung, nice to meet you in person," I said, and we shook hands. We'd spoken on the phone earlier that week to go over my testimony. I set down my notes, Leung got out a legal pad, and we sat down. He read me the questions he planned to ask and I recited the replies I planned to give. In court, attorneys never ask a question to which they don't already know the answer. While a TV staple, surprises are unwelcome.

Lastly, Leung asked me the "current mental illness" questions. I voiced my misgivings.

"I'm not telling you what to do," Leung said. "But you might think about keeping that to yourself. Unless you want Mr. McCoy to walk out of here a free man."

CHAPTER SIXTEEN

> *Sex is one of my downfalls. I get it any way I can. If I have to force somebody to do it, I do . . . I've killed animals to have sex with them, and I've had sex while they're alive.*
>
> **—Henry Lee Lucas, America's most prolific killer. Believed to have murdered 350 people between the years 1975 and 1983. His Texas death sentence was commuted by then governor George W. Bush. Lucas died in prison on March 12, 2001, of natural causes.**

Mental-health court cases work this way: The patient has been charged with a crime. When they first meet with their attorney, the lawyer voices a concern about the person's mental state either then or at the time of the alleged offense. Once raised, the insanity issue is referred to a court-appointed psychiatrist—called an alienist—for an opinion on the defendant's psychiatric diagnosis, his current mental condition, or his mental state at the time of the crime.

If, in the alienist's opinion, a person was mentally ill when he committed his crime and, because of his mental illness, didn't know right from wrong, then the public defender may ask a court to rule the person not guilty by reason of insanity (NGRI). This step isn't taken lightly. Should a judge rule a defendant NGRI, then they're found not guilty and sent to a state mental hospital for treatment. And not guilty means not guilty. The criminal part of the case is over. The charges are dropped. Treatment becomes the sole issue.

And as the Supreme Court delineated, the focus of this treatment isn't symptom relief, it's dangerousness. To maintain an NGRI commitment, the hospital must prove—on a regular basis—that a patient continues to suffer from a mental illness and that they're dangerous because of that mental illness. Being just mentally ill isn't enough, nor is just being dangerous.

Bill McCoy had been found NGRI. Despite the horrific nature of his crime, he was facing no charges. If Leung and I couldn't prove him currently mentally ill and dangerous because of it, he was going to go free.

Leung turned toward me. "I know this hearing puts you in a difficult situation," he said. "Mr. McCoy is your patient and I understand that giving testimony against him is troublesome. But I have to think about the people out there." He nodded to a nearby window. "They count on us for protection." We didn't speak for a moment.

"We'd better head down," Leung said finally. He hoisted a battered briefcase and held an arm to the door. We passed through a sparse crowd outside the courtroom.

I took a seat in the audience section. Leung walked through a small gate that separated the court proper from the spectators, set his briefcase beneath one of two tables in front of the judge's bench, and sat down.

As the spectator seats began to fill, I reread my notes. I thought about Unit C. I thought about McCoy. And about what Leung had said. I gazed out a small window. Across the street, two women jogged by.

There are two types of mental health proceedings: a "court"

trial, in which only a judge presides, and a jury trial. Mental health defendants can request either one. McCoy had asked for a jury trial.

In addition to mandated court reviews, a state hospital patient, like any person under state incarceration, is entitled to file, once a year, a writ of habeas corpus. *Writ* means "legal action." *Habeas corpus,* based on Old English law, means "produce the body." A writ of habeas corpus requires any detaining facility, in our case the hospital, to appear in court with a patient to have the legality of their continued detention examined. McCoy had filed a writ of habeas corpus. We were proceeding that morning with a writ hearing.

The mechanics of most hearings are pretty much the same. The interests of the hospital are represented by the county district attorney, who argues for a patient's continued detention. The defense attorney or public defender, also a county employee, argues for a patient's release. I am always called as a witness for the DA.

There are two types of witnesses: a witness of fact and an expert witness. A witness of fact can tell only what they saw or heard. An expert witness may give an opinion and draw conclusions. I was an expert witness. The DA would ask me questions first and then the public defender would cross-examine.

Mental health hearings are given no special place in the daily proceedings of a Superior Court schedule. That day I had to wait two hours for a dozen other cases—drug arrests, spousal abuse, assault and battery—to be adjudicated. Then the judge, a smallish woman with a no-nonsense manner, picked up her daily schedule, peered down, and said, "The case of William McCoy."

We waited while the bailiff walked down the aisle that split the audience seats and opened the door out into the corridor. Twelve jurors, selected the previous day, entered and took seats in the jury box to the judge's right, passing the attorneys who sat at the tables in front of the bench.

The bailiff opened a side door, and, escorted by two uniformed officers, McCoy entered the room. Shackled in ankle and wrist manacles and clad in clean blue scrubs, he shuffled slowly to a seat beside his attorney. He didn't look at me. A large skin-colored Band-Aid patch covered the *HELL* tattoo on his forehead.

"Is the state ready to proceed, Mr. Leung?" the judge asked.

"Yes, Your Honor," Leung said.

"Is the defense ready, Ms. McCarthy?" the judge continued.

"Yes, Your Honor," Susan McCarthy, a young woman in a dark pantsuit, said.

"Mr. Leung, call your first witness," the judge said.

Leung stood, turned, and said, "The state calls Dr. Seager."

I was glad for the extra two hours afforded by the preceding cases. It gave me a chance to carefully review my notes but, more importantly, it provided an opportunity to reconsider what I thought was fair, what I felt was my responsibility to Bill McCoy, to myself, and to the people outside the hospital.

It wasn't until I heard my name called, in fact, that my decision became clear. I rose and walked to the witness stand.

I stood to the judge's left, next to the witness box.

"Raise your right hand," the bailiff said, and I did.

Then the bailiff stated, "Do you solemnly swear that the testimony you are about to give in this matter is the truth, the whole truth, and nothing but the truth, so help you God?"

"Yes."

"Please be seated," the judge said.

I entered the witness box and sat down. A small pitcher of water, a plastic cup, and a Kleenex box had been placed to my left on a ledge out of view of the jury and spectators. Attached to the witness box railing was a microphone, which I adjusted.

"Please state your name and spell it," the bailiff said. As I did, a court reporter busily typed. I glanced at her, then quickly at the jury, the twelve faces—five men and seven women—who would decide the fate of Bill McCoy. I didn't look at McCoy, but I knew he was looking at me.

I turned as Leung rose. "Dr. Seager, what is your occupation?"

What followed was a standard set of questions and replies called voir dire, a phrase of uncertain etymology that has come to mean the practice of questioning prospective jurors for any potential bias or, in my case, testing the qualifications of a witness before they're certified as an "expert."

Leung's questions were straightforward and over with quickly. McCarthy's questions were not. "Where did you attend high school?" she began. And for the next thirty minutes, I answered questions about where I'd lived, what college classes I'd taken, what specific medical courses had been part of my curriculum, my grades for each class, and then, in detail, a description of my psychiatric training and all my previous jobs.

The questions were tedious and exhaustive. But I understood their purpose. I knew McCarthy would certify me as an expert witness. I was the only witness being called in the case. But her professional charge was to represent McCoy to the best of her ability. She knew the jurors were listening to her questions. And if during voir dire she could find even the smallest chink in my armor, it would be a mark in her favor.

"You've only worked at Napa State Hospital for six months?" McCarthy asked, and glanced at her notes for effect.

"Yes."

"Is that long enough to qualify you as an expert in this complicated matter?"

"Yes."

McCarthy set down her notes. "I'll accept Dr. Seager as an expert," she concluded.

McCoy had been paying particular attention to McCarthy's inquiries. He now knew a lot more about me than I felt comfortable with. He smiled at McCarthy, who gave him a faint nod.

Leung stood and the true hearing began. He asked me all the questions we'd rehearsed over the phone and again in his office. I gave a history of McCoy's behavior since I'd come to Unit C. The conversation became very specific when we covered the assault on Mr. Wilkins.

"You stated that you saw Mr. McCoy bash Mr. Wilkins over the head with a heavy wooden chair?" Leung asked.

"Objection," McCarthy said. "To use of the word *bash*."

"Sustained," the judge said.

Leung repeated his question. "You stated that you saw Mr. McCoy strike Mr. Wilkins over the head with a heavy wooden chair?"

"Yes," I answered.

"And weren't you also injured by Mr. McCoy as well?"

"Yes. He pushed my head into a wall. I received ten stitches."

Leung turned a page on his yellow legal pad and let that last sentence simmer.

"Have you formed an opinion concerning Mr. McCoy's psychiatric diagnosis?" Leung continued.

"Yes," I said.

"And what is that diagnosis?"

"Bipolar disorder, manic with psychotic features."

"That's bullshit and he knows it!" McCoy roared, and the jury collectively flinched.

The judge banged down her gavel. "Ms. McCarthy, you will instruct your client to refrain from any more outbursts," she said. "Or I will have him removed from the courtroom."

McCarthy turned and spoke heatedly to McCoy. He quieted but it took a moment. "I'm sorry, Your Honor," McCarthy said. "It won't happen again."

The judge nodded to Leung.

"And upon what do you base that diagnosis?" Leung asked.

"Mr. McCoy has a history of severe mood swings and of hearing voices," I said.

"Are those symptoms in evidence currently?" Leung asked.

"No."

"Have they been in evidence during the past six months?"

"Yes."

"If I produced Mr. McCoy's hospital chart," Leung said, "could you show me where these symptoms are documented?"

"Yes."

McCoy whispered to McCarthy, who didn't turn her head.

Leung walked back to his table, pulled a red Gomorrah chart from atop a small stack of papers, paced back, and handed it to me.

I found the correct page. "May I read?" I asked.

"Please," Leung said.

"From a nursing note dated the day of Mr. McCoy's assault on Mr. Wilkins," I began, and read verbatim from the chart. " 'After the attack, Mr. McCoy stated—grabbing his head—"The voices made me do it," then he walked into the courtyard.' "

McCarthy clamped a hand on McCoy's arm to keep him from jumping up. They exchanged words quietly.

"Your witness," Leung said, and sat down.

McCarthy made certain McCoy was under wraps before she stood.

"Is there anywhere else in Mr. McCoy's chart," she stated calmly, "where any other symptoms of psychosis are documented?"

"No."

"That chart is fairly thick," McCarthy said. "Dr. Seager, could you please hold it up for the jury to see?"

I held up the chart and turned it sideways so everyone could appreciate the four inches of paper it contained.

"And in that entire chart," McCarthy went on, "there is only one entry that you claim documents Mr. McCoy's alleged ongoing psychosis?"

"Yes."

McCarthy stepped toward me. "Is it possible that statement was meant as a joke?"

"Nothing that awful day was a joke," I said.

"You were there, of course?"

"Yes."

"Did you hear Mr. McCoy utter those words?" McCarthy said.

"Yes, I did."

"Did you take his statement to mean he was really hearing voices?" McCarthy said.

I faced McCarthy directly. "I don't know what he meant," I said. "I just know what he said."

McCarthy stared at the sheaf of notes in her hand; then she glanced at the jury, then back at me. "No further questions," she said.

"You're excused, Dr. Seager," the judge said.

I wasn't expected to stay for the remainder of the case. The court would, no doubt, hear from McCoy, and then Leung and McCarthy would sum up, after which the jury would decide McCoy's fate. But my part was over.

I walked past Leung's table, through the small swinging gate, down the spectator aisle, and out the courtroom door. I got into my truck and headed toward the interstate. Storm clouds were gathering.

CHAPTER SEVENTEEN

[He] started messing with the Christmas tree, telling me how nice the Christmas tree was. So I shot him.

—David Bullock, who killed six people in 1981–82. Victim number five was Heriberto Morales, age fifty, who visited Bullock's home after a Christmas party.

On Monday morning, I gathered my courage and opened the door to Unit C. Every morning that week would be the same. And every morning, my relief was measurable when McCoy's bed lay tightly made and empty. By Friday I started to relax. "They must have let him go," I thought, driving home.

I spent the weekend with Ingrid and John getting ready for Christmas. We shopped. We wrapped gifts. We ate out. John and I strung tiny icicle lights from the house eaves and hauled home the largest, most fragrant Douglas fir tree we could find.

Driving to work on Monday, I checked off a list of last-minute gifts I'd yet to order from Amazon. *Christmas isn't until Sunday,* I thought. *No problem.*

I cruised through the sally port, walked the green yard, passed a clutch of idling peacocks, and headed to my office. Emails read, I walked to Unit C.

I turned the lock. The hallway was empty. I walked toward the nurses' station.

"Merry Christmas," McCoy called from his room, and poked his head into the hallway. Bandage gone, *HELL* was back. "Nice to see you, Dr. Seager."

"Nice to see you, Mr. McCoy," I said. Walking to rounds proved difficult.

"McCoy's back," I said, and sat down.

"He looked fine to me," Hancock reassured.

"You never know with these guys," Xiang countered. "That's the problem."

"Don't worry," Cohen said. "We've got your back."

"I'm not worried," I lied. "Let's begin."

At the end of rounds, I still felt uncomfortable. "Could we please talk to McCoy?" I said. "I need to know how he feels about this court business."

"Good idea," Xiang said, and everyone agreed.

"I'll get him," Cohen said, and left the room.

We sat in silence until the conference room door opened again.

"Morning, all," McCoy said, and took a seat across the table from me and Cohen.

"Good morning, Mr. McCoy," Xiang replied.

"What'd I do wrong?" McCoy asked. "The team never asks to see me."

"We just wanted to check in and see how you're doing," Cohen said. "We know court didn't go like you'd hoped. We wondered how you were feeling?"

"I'm all right," McCoy said.

"I testified against you, Mr. McCoy," I said. "Are you okay with that?"

McCoy looked at me intently. For an instant, I thought he might jump across the table.

"Mr. McCoy . . . ?" Xiang said. "Are you okay with that?"

"Ah, sure, I'm all right," McCoy said finally, and smiled. "I understand you were just doing your job, Doc. Hell, that's not the first time I've been to court. Probably won't be the last."

Then his smile waned. "I'm not saying I agree with what you said," McCoy continued. "And I don't think you quite believed it, either." He flicked his shoulders. "But what's done is done."

"Court is difficult for everyone," Cohen said. "But I want to ask you directly: are you planning any revenge? Are you going to hurt someone?"

"That's not my style," McCoy said.

"What is your style?" I asked.

McCoy sat back. "You may not believe this," he said, "but I used to be one of you guys. I used to wear a suit and tie to work. I've been to college. I was a certified public accountant. I had a wife. Owned a house. The whole nine yards. Hell, Doc," he continued, "I used to teach CPR at the YMCA. Weird, huh? CPR? A fucking accountant? At least until I was introduced to Mr. Methamphetamine." He laughed.

"An accountant," Hancock said. "That's interesting."

I had no idea where we were heading.

"My specialty was business accounting," McCoy continued. "It's truly a beautiful thing. Do you know why? Because at the end of the day, or the week or the year or sometimes even a decade, the books always get balanced. You owe, you pay."

"Is that a threat?" I asked.

"Threat, Doc?" McCoy replied slowly. "Nah, I was just talking about accounting."

"You gave Dr. Seager ten stitches in his head," Cohen said. "I think the books are balanced."

"Ten stitches for another year in here?" McCoy said.

Tired of feeling scared, I squared up. "Mr. McCoy," I said, "forget the stitches. Let me tell you about something I read. It's about a new law coming out of the state legislature called 'guilty but insane.' Have you heard about it?"

McCoy looked a hair off center. "Something like that, yeah. I've heard about it," he said.

"It means that if a person commits a violent crime," I said, "like an assault, even if they were insane at the time, they'd do their full sentence in prison, not here. Prison, where they don't have a softball league." I sat back, as McCoy had earlier. "And the law is going to be retroactive to last September."

McCoy straightened. We locked eyes and didn't waver.

"Don't want to miss out on softball," McCoy finally said, and looked away.

THERE ARE TWO types of threats. A "hot" threat is made in the pitch of anger: "I'm going to kill you!" It's obvious and right there. A "cold" threat is calculated and cool: "The books always get balanced." A cold threat can easily be denied. It might even seem innocuous. But they're very real and eminently more dangerous. Anger settles, but ice waits.

Cohen took McCoy back to his room. Everyone looked at me.

"Very good," Hancock said.

"I agree," Palanqui stated.

"We'll keep an eye out just the same," Xiang said.

Cohen came back. “McCoy was asking all about that new law you talked about,” he said. “Where'd you read that?”

“Online, I think. I'll look for the link,” I said.

Exhausted and hoping to change the subject, I turned to Palanqui. “Did I hear something about Santa visiting the hospital?”

Palanqui brightened. “Every year. The last Friday before Christmas. This Friday afternoon, in fact.”

“What happens?” Cohen had perked up as well.

“You'll see,” Xiang said.

I knew any reprieve I'd bought from McCoy was only temporary. He had people outside the fence. They could use the Internet. But at least, I figured, I'd probably be okay for the holidays.

On Tuesday afternoon I stood in the Unit C hallway. An older man walked up. “Merry Christmas,” he said. “I made this for you in Craft Class.” He handed me a colorfully painted wooden stick adorned with red and silver glitter. “It's a shamanistic trick phone,” he stated confidently.

“Thank you,” I said, and put the gift just inside the nurses' station door on a small window ledge. “This way everyone can see it.”

On Wednesday, Burns wheeled by my side. “For you,” he said, and held up a small watercolor.

I admired it in the hallway light. It was a mix of red and green. “It's a . . .”

“Christmas ornament on a tree,” Burns said. “It was my favorite when I was a kid.”

“Beautifully done,” I stated. “Merry Christmas, Mr. Burns.” He smiled and pushed away. The picture went next to the spangled stick.

Gifts from a patient to a psychiatrist are always laden with meaning and generally frowned upon. On an inpatient unit, they stir up issues of favoritism or quid pro quo, both of which must be assiduously avoided. Hurt feelings or paranoid misinterpretation can lead to violence.

The rules of separation between psychiatrists and patients have evolved over the years and are now strict. No emotional entanglement. No financial ties. No physical contact. No favors. No presents, etc. The line separating a patient and doctor is called the boundary, and any breach of protocol is referred to as a boundary violation. Almost every psychiatrist who loses their license goes down a path that began with a boundary violation.

On Thursday, Tom Caruthers waved me over to his room. He had a small package wrapped neatly in construction paper pilfered from the art studio. "It's not a gift," he said, and put the thin package in my hand. "I'm just returning something."

I took the package and a lump formed in my throat. I knew exactly what was inside.

"You gave it to me when I was in high school," Caruthers said. "And it helped me through some stuff. Each time I saw it I thought of you and how I didn't want to let you down."

I peeled up two strips of tape and folded open the paper. Inside, encased in a clear plastic sleeve, was a 1959 Sandy Koufax baseball card. Caruthers and I had both been big baseball fans. And I'd always loved baseball cards. I'd given the Koufax card to Caruthers back when boundary issues weren't so clear.

A hundred memories flooded back. About Caruthers when he was young. About me when I was young. And about my father when he'd given the card to me. I stared at it.

"You know I can't accept this," I said.

"I know," Caruthers replied. "But it's helped me all it can. You'll find someone who needs it."

He took my hands in his. "Merry Christmas," he said, and went back into his room.

I knew exactly what to do with the long-forgotten card. Boundary violations aside, I put it in my pocket.

"WE'LL FORM UP at three," Larsen said after Friday rounds. "And walk the guys down to the parade."

"A parade?" I asked.

"Santa's coming," Monabong said. "You have to have a parade."

"He's traveled a long way," Cohen added. "He expects it."

"Who's playing Santa this year?" Palanqui asked.

"Mr. Watson from upstairs," Xiang said.

"Watson?" Palanqui chimed in. "He's just a little bitty guy." She held her hand out at shoulder height.

"He's the only man all year," Xiang said, "without an alarm incident."

After lunch, Cohen and I passed Palanqui and Monabong heading toward the sally port. They wore green felt elf costumes with red striped socks, pointy hats, and curled shoes. We waved. They did a spontaneous elf dance and waved back.

In the center of the STA, on a large patch of green fronting the D Units, a wooden stage had been erected. On top of it stood a twenty-foot Christmas tree, decorated with dozens of big white-and-blue papier-mâché ornaments and three thick, twining ropes of silver bunting. A canvas tree skirt circled the bottom, and a pile of brightly painted, outsize wooden boxes topped with enormous colored bows lay on the skirt. To the right of the tree was a podium and behind that two rows of folding chairs.

Back on the unit, Cohen and I joined the rest of the staff and most of the Unit C men; a few patients elected to remain behind and two night nurses had agreed to stay with them. Xiang checked everyone's name off a list, then Cohen unlocked the door and we headed out.

I walked with Boudreaux while Caruthers pushed Ortega behind us. The rest of the staff wandered ahead, interspersed among the other Unit C men. From across the campus, like streams collecting in a storm, patients flowed toward the giant green tree. A large crowd gathered in front of the stage.

Like Christmas anywhere, everyone was excited. Unlike Christmas anywhere else, a full-force police presence encircled the revelers. "White Christmas" and "Rudolph, the Red-Nosed Reindeer" rang out from speakers appended to nearby tree trunks. People sang along. Finally, Dr. Francis rose and tapped a microphone on the thin lectern.

"Welcome to Napa State Hospital's annual Christmas celebration," she said. "Is everyone having a good time?"

A general "Yeah" rang out.

Dr. Francis thanked the hospital dignitaries on hand, then the workers who'd done the stage construction and tree decoration. "Without further ado," she said, "Marla Castle from the women's unit will light our official Napa State tree."

A large white woman with short-cropped brown hair stood next to Dr. Francis.

"Let's count down," Dr. Francis said. "Five, four, three . . ." she called, and the crowd echoed. Just after "three," Castle excitedly threw the lever and the tree exploded in light.

". . . Two, one," Dr. Francis concluded but was drowned out by a collective gasp and applause.

Dr. Francis turned and pointed toward the sally port. "I think our guest of honor has arrived."

Onto the main drag pulled two immaculately restored 1958 long-finned Cadillac convertibles, each driven by a smiling policeman. Green-clad elves stood and waved from the gleaming blue car in front. In the trailing pink vehicle, seated on top of the backseat, rode a very small Santa in full regalia. Beside him lay his bag of toys. The PA system played "Here Comes Santa Claus."

The patients hopped and craned for a closer look. "Let's give Santa a big Napa State welcome," Dr. Francis boomed.

The crowd erupted in a sustained cheer as Santa and his elves wended their way toward the dais. The elves emerged from the first car and formed two lines alongside the second. Santa exited the pink car (or at least seemed to, I could just see the top of his hat moving among the elves. It looked like a red ball bouncing along a green felt tabletop).

Santa mounted two wooden steps and appeared on the stage with his bag. Dr. Francis walked over to formally welcome him, and then she looked at the crowd and held out her arm, nearly poking Santa in the eye. Standing next to Dr. Francis, Santa looked like a gaily dressed schoolboy.

Then Santa stopped, stood straight, and turned abruptly. He stared into the crowd and pointed. "Hey," he shouted suddenly. "Keep your hands off my girl!"

"Fuck you, Santa," shouted a big man in the front row, his arms draped around a dark-haired woman.

Santa picked up his toy bag, slung it over his shoulder, and marched to the front of the stage. "Fuck me? Fuck you!" he bellowed.

"Shut up, shrimp," the big man replied.

Santa twisted around, winding his toy bag for a swing.

Cohen pulled his alarm. "Let's go," he shouted, and we jumped onto the platform. Xiang tackled Santa just as he gave his bag a mighty heave. The sack clipped Cohen on top of the head and everyone fell into a writhing jumble. Cops filled the stage and quickly restored order.

"You no-good, two-timing slut!" Santa shouted. He continued to wrestle but was no match for Cohen and Xiang. I grabbed Santa's bag. It was filled with laundry.

Four cops pulled Santa up and carried him toward the back of the stage, his feet kicking. Amid the confusion, some of the tree lights went out, two big packages tumbled to the ground and got kicked, and a long strand of silver bunting slid down and sloshed between rustling feet. As the dignitaries filed away, a chair tipped over.

The cops and staff walked the patients back to their respective units. I fell in with the Unit C group. We'd gone a bit when I noticed that Cervantes, raccoon mask intact, pink flags bobbing, was walking behind me.

I stepped to the side and let him pass. Unnerved, I searched for McCoy but couldn't see him. I let everyone go by until I was alone. Then I went back to help clean up the mess.

CHAPTER EIGHTEEN

While I was sitting there, a little kid about eleven or twelve years old came bumming around. He was looking for something. He found it too. I took him out to a gravel pit . . . I left him there, but first I committed sodomy on him, then killed him. His brains were coming out of his ears when I left him.

—Carl Panzram, who admitted to killing twenty-one people, including six African guides on a crocodile hunt. He cut them up and fed them to the crocodiles. Panzram was hanged September 5, 1930.

My mood brightened when I saw Amazon packages on the hall table. John eyed them. "What are you looking at?" I said, and smiled.

"Just taking inventory," John said. "I need to plan out the space in my room."

"Sure they're for you?" I said, then collected the pile and headed to the bedroom.

"They're from Amazon," John replied. "They're not for Mom."

"When did you get so smart?" I called out.

Christmas Eve arrived. I knew Ingrid was a little down without her family around. Next year it was our turn for the big holiday—Ingrid's parents and all the brothers and sisters, nieces and nephews, would be at our home. But this year, it was just us three and the dogs.

On Christmas Eve, we trimmed the tree and exchanged gifts.

The last gift was a small rectangle of silver wrapping paper. John picked it up and read the tag. "To John. Much love, Dad."

"You guys are always Santa," John said.

"This is something a little different," I said. Ingrid looked at me quizzically.

John carefully undid the paper and slid out a hard plastic protector, which housed the 1959 Sandy Koufax baseball card Caruthers had given me.

"My father gave the card to me when I was young," I said. "When I first became a psychiatrist, I gave it to someone very close to me. Now he's grown and he gave it back. And now I'm giving it to the person I love the most."

"Koufax," John said. "He's famous, right?"

"He's the best pitcher in baseball history," I said. "I saw him pitch once when I was a kid. I actually thought his card had special power. Like it gave me some kind of protection. It helped me through my parents' divorce."

"You never told me that," Ingrid said.

"I was a dumb kid," I said.

"I love it," John said. "Whoever he is."

ON UNIT C, the week between Christmas and New Year's passed without event. We had a few minor scuffles but nothing too bad. People talked about Santa's visit, which never failed to bring a laugh. The story was now part of the parallel universe of Gomorrah lore, the kind where no one got hurt and you felt something besides dread.

McCoy and I passed each other in the hallway a time or two. He was respectful. I gave him a wide berth. Cervantes left me alone as well. I planned to make one New Year's resolution: to not have any more patients want to kill me.

"What are you doing for New Year's Eve?" Hancock asked. We were the last people to leave rounds that Friday.

"We have something with my wife's work," I said. "How about you?"

"The family's going to church," Hancock said. "It's what we do. We're cooking meals at the homeless shelter the next day."

"No football?" I asked.

"Nothing against football," she said. "We'll be back in front of the TV next Monday night."

"May I ask what church your family belongs to?"

"We're Seventh-day Adventists," Hancock said.

"Millerites."

"Indeed."

"My son went to an Adventist school in fourth grade," I said. "It was a great year."

"I'm glad to hear that," Hancock said.

"Can I make a small donation to the shelter?" I asked. "Maybe help with the meals?"

"A donation would be wonderful."

After losing it for the umpteenth time, I'd stopped carrying a wallet a few years back. I pulled some bills out of my front pocket, straightened them, and handed the pack to Hancock. I didn't count nor did she.

"Who's your team in the weekend bowl games?" Hancock asked, and put the cash in her jeans pocket.

"Utah. I'm from there."

Hancock patted her pocket. "This is good for at least a touchdown," she said.

I stayed late to get my computer work done before the long New Year's weekend. After texting Ingrid, I checked my email a final time, shut down the computer, locked the office, donned my winter jacket, and headed out the main door.

I pulled up the jacket collar against the cold. I hadn't walked fifty feet, however, when a sickening déjà vu stopped me dead.

To my right, behind Unit C, another cigarette buy was going down. One person passed a carton to another and money went the other way. It was the same cone of light. The same murky figures. But I wasn't the same.

I pulled my hip alarm and a siren blared. The two figures startled. One dropped the money, the other the cigarettes. They scrambled behind the building and disappeared into the night.

Headlights zoomed up the main drag. The Unit C door opened and a phalanx of staff charged out. Two cop cars slammed to a halt and the doors blew open. I waved everyone over. My pulse was normal.

"You okay, Doc?" Cole asked when he recognized me. Three other cops were with him, red and blue lights pulsing behind them.

"I'm fine," I assured Cole as staff from Units C and B arrived. I clicked off the alarm.

"We knew you'd just left the building," Palanqui said between cloudy breaths. "The alarm scared the shit out of us." A nurse and two psych techs from Unit B nodded.

"I'm fine," I said. "But that's not." I pointed to the deserted area behind Unit C.

"Someone sold a carton of cigarettes," I said. "The alarm freaked them. They dropped everything and took off." On the ground lay a carton of Marlboro Red cigarettes and a wad of bills held together by a rubber band.

"Which way?" Cole said.

I pointed. "Behind the building."

"I'll track 'em on foot," Cole shouted, and gestured to the other cops. "You guys start behind the D buildings and search the fence perimeter." The three cops leaped into their vehicles and screeched away.

"Stay put," Cole said to the assembled staff. He trotted behind Unit C.

We stood quietly for a few seconds. The nurses looked at one another. "We'd better get back," Palanqui said. "The police seem to have things under control."

"Good idea," I said.

"You going to be all right?" a Unit B tech asked.

"The cops are on it," I replied. "We'd just be in the way."

"Happy New Year, Doc," Palanqui said, and the staff walked away.

"Same to you," I said, and heard another siren.

A third police car, lights ablaze, rolled to a stop. Someone got out and walked toward me.

"You again?" Detective Levin said.

"I saw another cigarette buy. Cole ran that way." I pointed. "He's going to need all the help he can get."

"Cole can handle himself," Levin said. "I'm more interested in why you're always—"

"Detective!" a cop suddenly yelled from an open window as his cruiser raced up and skidded to a stop.

"Over behind the D Units," he sputtered, his face blurred with cloudy breath.

Levin and I sprinted away.

We jogged a few hundred feet to the edge of the D complex and turned behind the buildings along a delivery alley that circled in back. In the center of the alley, opposite a concrete loading pad and truck bay, Cole stood at the back fence line. He shone a flashlight along the top of the fence, illuminating a ten-foot span without razor wire.

"It's for delivery trucks," Cole said. "They can't get in otherwise."

"No one's supposed to know about that," Levin said.

"If the perps ran behind here," Cole said, and scanned around the empty grounds, "you can bet that's where they went up and over."

"Call in backup," Levin said to another cop. "I'll get the county sheriff on the horn. We'll need a complete perimeter search."

"Including helicopters?" the other cop asked.

"Including helicopters," Levin replied.

"Get some tape and cordon off this area," Cole said. "And secure the section behind Unit C as well." He shook his head. "Jesus, I didn't think anyone could get out of here."

"Officer Cole, I'll meet you at the sally port," Levin said. "Alert all the hospital units that we have a patient over the wall. And get administration on the line; they'll need to order a bed check."

"How do you know it was a patient?" I asked.

"Who else would buy cigarettes inside the fence?" Levin said.

Cole jumped in his cruiser and sped off.

Levin gazed up at the moonlit sky, then back at me and sighed. "Why are you always around when these things happen?" he said.

Two helicopters darted above, a cluster of police cruisers raked the fence line, and an army of cops—hospital and Napa city—

walked the Gomorrah campus. Inside the hospital police station, appended to the sally port, I gave Levin a detailed statement concerning what I'd seen.

"What was the first person wearing?"

"I'm not sure. It was dark."

"What color was their hair?"

"Again, it was dark."

"You said there were two people inside the fence?"

"Yes."

"It wasn't too dark for that?"

I kept my cool. "I saw two people inside the fence," I said.

"Are you certain there weren't more?"

"No, but I only saw two."

And so it went. Finally finished with me, Levin gave a summary to his boss, Chief Erickson, and two local detectives in suits. While the Unit C nurses and the Unit B techs gave their accounts, I took the time to call Ingrid and let her know what happened and that I was okay. I told her not to wait up.

"Don't talk about this to anyone," Levin said, bringing the interviews to a close. "Nothing leaves this room. Understand?" The last part wasn't really a question.

"Got it," I said.

When I finally got home it was midnight. In the bedroom, Ingrid sat in a chair.

"Are you okay?" she said, and stood.

"I'm fine," I replied, and gave her a hug.

"A patient escaped?" Ingrid said.

"Looks like it."

Ingrid startled. "That's terrible. Did they find him?"

"Not yet," I said. I sat on the side of the bed and slipped off my shoes. "But it wasn't for lack of trying. I think every cop in town is there. You must have heard the helicopters?"

"I did," Ingrid said. "So did John."

I sighed.

"Can't they just run a patient census and see who's missing?" Ingrid asked.

"That'll take a day or two," I said. "The hospital has twelve hundred beds, people are on home visits, and some are at County General. There are discharges and admits."

"They don't know how many people are in the hospital?" Ingrid said.

"Of course they do," I said, backtracking. "They'll find him."

I didn't tell Ingrid that the census issue was an ongoing problem at Gomorrah. Rarely did anyone know exactly how many people were in the hospital. I had patients on my "official" hospital computer roster who had left the hospital months ago.

"You were gone a long time," Ingrid said.

"I pulled the alarm. I saw everything. The cops had lots of questions."

Ingrid grew quiet. "Are we safe?" she finally asked.

"Of course," I replied.

"This escaped person probably knows you, right?" she said. "You said this all happened outside your unit. Can he find out where we live?"

"It's probably over by now," I said reassuringly. All the way home I'd wondered the same thing.

Neither Ingrid nor I slept well. We woke early and checked the morning paper. Despite the massive police response and helicopters circling the night sky, we found no mention of a patient escape, no mention of Gomorrah at all. We listened to the news. Same result.

"A state mental hospital patient escapes," Ingrid said, "and we hear nothing? How could anything be more dangerous?"

That evening I slipped on my coat and joined John on the porch. "I'll go with you," I said. It was just dark. He was headed to his friend Sean Hansen's house to spend the night.

"It's only two blocks," John said as we turned down the sidewalk.

"I can use the air," I said.

"Is this about the guy who escaped from your hospital?" John said.

"Where did you hear that?"

"I'll be fine, Dad," John said. "Don't worry."

I dropped John at the Hansens' door, made small talk with Sean's parents, then walked home.

"Should we be going to a party tonight?" Ingrid said when I stepped in the door.

"It's important for your work," I said. "We have to go. I won't let these lunatics ruin my home life, too."

Ingrid smiled. "Besides," she said, "who'd look for us there?"

A dozen other couples attended the affair—a New Year's Eve party hosted by a physician colleague of Ingrid's—all of whom knew her and none of whom knew me. This meant introductions and answers to the question "What do you do?"

People have two reactions to my job. One is a look of momentary horror and a slight pullback, as if I might be contagious. The other is a flash of piqued interest followed by a conspiratorial smile. Then comes a version of the same question: "Do you have any mastermind patients, evil-genius types? You know, who're smarter than the staff and it's all you can do to keep one step ahead of them?"

My feelings about these reactions are conflicted. I understand the people who recoil. Who wouldn't? But the second response—or, more precisely, my reaction to the second response—bothers me. In an honest moment, I had to confess that despite everything, Gomorrah was exciting. And admitting that was difficult.

I DREAMED OF Detective Levin. We were back in the sally port room. It was close and hot. Levin loomed large. Leaning in, he peppered me with questions. My answers echoed down a canyon. He spoke faster and faster. His voice rang. He sprayed me with spit. And then I'd finally had enough. I punched him in the mouth.

CHAPTER NINETEEN

> *"She looks like the type that might freak out. It's something in the eyes, Frannie. It says if you shoot my sacred cows, I'll shoot yours."*
>
> —Stephen King, *The Stand*

A new year meant a new start. I went to work early to clean up some paperwork. Walking onto the unit at seven thirty, I discovered that despite the new start, we still had the same old faces and the same old problems.

"You stupid son of a bitch," Oliver Burns yelled as Mathews grabbed Burns's wheelchair handles and raced him full speed down the entire length of the deserted hallway. Mathews laughed out loud and barely skidded to a stop in front of the far wall. Burns whipsawed forward and back.

Mathews slapped Burns on the back of the head and walked away.

"You lousy fucking bastard, I'll kill you!" Burns screamed, and righted his chair.

Nearby staff members gathered. "Are you okay, Mr. Burns?" I said.

Burns pushed past us. "You can all go fuck yourselves," he spat. "And take Mathews with you."

"Mr. Mathews is a first-class jerk," Palanqui fumed. "One day he'll get his."

"How long has this been going on?" I asked.

"Mr. Mathews began the wheelchair business this weekend," a night nurse said. "But he's always doing something awful."

I walked down the hallway to check on Burns.

"May I talk to you, Mr. Burns?" I said from just inside his doorway. Burns sat in front of the window looking out into the courtyard.

"Eat me," he said, and didn't move.

COMING IN EARLY meant I'd driven to work in the dark. I hadn't noticed the storm clouds. But as we prepared for rounds, the skies opened and it poured rain.

The staff stood near a window outside the conference room.

"I hear it's gonna be a bad one," Monabong said as rain pelted the glass. "News called it 'The Pineapple Express.' They said to expect tons of heavy tropical rain."

"Hope it's not like '06," Larsen said.

"What happened in '06?" I asked.

"Our building is old," Xiang said. "Drainage is not good. Water flooded the courtyard and hallways. Sandbags everywhere."

"The Napa River topped its banks," Randy said. "Downtown was under three feet of water. All the roads washed out. People couldn't get to work."

"Or leave," Monabong added. "If you were here, you stayed."

"It probably won't happen again," Xiang said. "But I'll call for sandbags anyway."

"We need to talk with Mathews," I said at the end of rounds. "He's harassing the wheelchair men at night."

"He almost killed Burns," Palanqui said.

"I'm certain talking to Mathews for the hundredth time will help," Cohen added.

Xiang looked over. "Any better idea?"

"We're all frustrated," Carstairs said. "I think talking to Mathews will help us as much as him."

Carstairs rarely spoke up. "Good point," I said.

Randy went to get Mathews. They entered and took seats at the table. Talking to Mathews went the way talking to Mathews usually went.

"We brought you in, Mr. Mathews," Cohen began, "because the night shift says you're harassing the wheelchair patients."

"That's a lie," Mathews said.

"I saw you do it," I interjected.

"Don't know what you saw, Doc," Mathews shot back, and glared at me. "But I ain't harassing nobody. It's all a lie. Everything is a lie."

It was a tight moment. Mathews was getting hot.

"We're not accusing you of anything, Mr. Mathews," Cohen said. "But could you please leave the wheelchair guys alone that you're not harassing?"

Mathews looked perplexed. But it worked. "Okay," Mathews said, and settled down.

"Thanks for your time," Xiang said. "Randy will walk you back."

Mathews left without incident. The door closed to a collective sigh of relief.

We prepared to stand, but before anyone could leave, I asked,

"Did a patient escape from the hospital Friday night?" I'd gone over different ways to bring up the subject, and the direct approach won.

"What?" Kate Henry said.

"I haven't heard anything," Cohen added. "What do you mean?"

Everyone looked startled.

"No one is missing from here," Xiang said.

I had a weird feeling. "Sorry," I said. "I thought something happened."

That afternoon, rain pummeling my office window, I flipped the computer on and checked my email. One message appeared, accompanied by a red exclamation mark. It was from hospital administration. I clicked and read: "A hospital-wide census completed this morning reveals that all Napa State Hospital beds are full. Proceed accordingly."

That night, as Ingrid stood before the bathroom sink, she asked if there was any news about the escape.

"Something happened," I replied. "But I'm not sure what. Hospital administration says all the beds are full."

"So no one escaped?" Ingrid asked, and turned.

"They didn't say that," I answered. "They just said all the beds were full."

"Didn't you see someone go over the fence?"

"Not exactly," I said. "But the cops were pretty sure that's what happened."

Ingrid didn't speak for a moment. "What are we supposed to do?" she said finally. "What do I tell John?"

"I don't know," I said.

Ingrid picked up her brush and turned again to the mirror. "People escape, they don't escape. You get hit. There are brawls. There are murders, for Christ's sake. What kind of hellhole do you work in?" she said, and pulled the brush through her hair. Ingrid rarely swore.

I looked at her in the mirror. "I wish I had an answer."

THE RAIN CONTINUED unabated, and driving to work became a serious challenge. News footage showed kayaks on flooded downtown streets. Each day I felt lucky to arrive at Gomorrah and even more so to get home.

On the unit, sandbags lay at the threshold to the courtyard. The water outside stood three inches deep and rising. Like Xiang said, we had an old building, and as the pelting continued, water began to seep in from windows and sills. A swath of my office wall became damp where a previously unseen crack now traced. Shoes squeaked on hall tiles. Mold bloomed.

And the smell returned. It erupted again in the hallway between Cohen's and my office, stopping me in my tracks. Cohen, walking by with Hancock and Palanqui, recoiled. "Not again."

"This one is particularly bad," Hancock said.

"Hasn't anybody ever gone up inside the ceiling and looked around?" Cohen asked.

"They've looked plenty," Hancock said. "Maintenance people went up into the rafters, combed the basement, and even tore open the wall once. But never found anything. So, I guess they just quit."

"Legend has it," Palanqui said, "like a hundred years ago, a patient was murdered and the body got plastered into the wall."

"They would have found something like that," I said.

"It's just a legend," Palanqui replied.

Hancock drifted over near a window that looked outside. Despite the rain, you could still see hills and trees in the distance.

"Back in the day," Hancock said, "the hospital grounds used to run from the river behind us all the way past those hills and around in each direction as far as you can see.

"There wasn't anything else out here then," she went on. "The hospital was isolated and self-sufficient. Patients did all the labor. They grew food. They cut timber. Hauled water. They made their own clothing. The staff lived here full-time as well. For years no one knew or cared what went on here." She turned. "Forget the wall, God knows what's buried out there."

THE WEEKEND ENDED; the rain didn't. I left home an hour early to navigate the flood that had become my drive to work. Cars littered small unpaved side roads. The parking lot flowed. The sally port now a lake, everyone entered on a tremulous plank walkway resting on cement blocks. The hospital grounds had become a waterfowl preserve.

The sudden appearance of a vast inland waterway brought ducks, geese, and swans from miles around. Umbrella in hand, I hopscotched from one dry spot to another as, by the scores, silken white birds glided gracefully past in all directions.

Water lapped the steps of the Unit C building. Hallways were muddy. A thin rill ran in front of my office.

I checked the expanding water mark on my wall and opened my computer. I had one email. It said "You are required to appear as a witness in an administrative Patient Rights hearing concerning the conduct of Officer Ted Cole." The hearing was set for twelve thirty that afternoon.

CHAPTER TWENTY

No matter how many pills
No matter how strong
No matter the cocktail of meds
I can't seem to be who they want.
—from "Medicine and Madness" by Josh C. DeWees

Every person admitted to a psychiatric hospital, whether voluntarily or involuntarily, has certain rights protected by law. This concept and the specific rights enumerated have evolved over time through a system of statutes, regulations, and court decisions.

The head of a psychiatric facility is responsible for seeing that each patient's rights are protected. A patient rights advocate from an independent Patient Rights Department is assigned to every hospital patient and is available to discuss any grievance anyone may have concerning a potential rights violation.

The advocate may also, if they deem an alleged infraction of adequate severity, convene a Patient Rights hearing to remediate the wrong. Staff penalties may result.

Every patient admitted to Gomorrah is given a *Patient Rights Handbook* in which their rights are detailed. The book is twenty-seven pages long.

The exact rights retained by every patient include:

> *The right to dignity, privacy, and humane care; the right to treatment; the right to refuse treatment; the right to receive care in the "least restrictive" setting; the right to be free of neglect, abuse, excessive restraint, isolation, or medication; the right to social activities, recreation, and physical exercise; the right to education; the right to religious freedom and practice; the right to be free from discrimination based upon race, color, religion, sex, national origin, ancestry, age, marital status, physical or mental disability, medical condition, or sexual orientation; the right to money, visitors every day, storage space, personal possessions, telephone access, unopened mail, writing materials, and stamps.*

The hearing to which I had been summoned concerned Officer Ted Cole and was based on an allegation by Mr. Alex Mathews that he'd been abused during the Unit C shakedown some months earlier. The proceedings were scheduled to take place in an administration building conference room. I slogged back across campus, over the sally port bridge, and around a dozen reservoirs of standing water.

The administration building had been a later addition to Gomorrah. Inside, it was warm and dry, and my shoes didn't squeak. I passed offices for the Patient Bank, Accounting, Medical Records, and Dr. Francis. Standing in front of a large wooden door, I checked the number I'd written on a slip of paper, then walked inside.

A long, gleaming conference table ran the entire length of the room. Upholstered chairs circled the table. I took a seat across from Dr. Francis. Beside her sat Charlene Larsen, dressed in street clothes. At the head of the table, a kind-faced, middle-aged woman nodded as I introduced myself.

"I'm Priscilla Hollenbeck," she said. "Head of the state Office of Patients' Rights."

"Ms. Hollenbeck flew down from Sacramento in this terrible weather," Dr. Francis said.

"Welcome to Napa State," I said.

Before Hollenbeck could respond, the door opened and Ted Cole walked in. He wore a dark blue suit and matching striped tie. His jacket was slightly too small. He was accompanied by a tall black man, wearing a suit as well. "Marvin Lipscomb, Hospital Police Association of California," he said, and took a seat next to Cole on the opposite side of the table. Lipscomb's organization, HPAC, was the statewide hospital police officers' union.

A round of introductions followed, and the door opened a final time. Mathews entered first. His hair neatly combed and his face freshly shaven, he wore newly pressed blue scrubs. "I'm Lorena Chen," a young Asian woman said, following behind. "Patient rights advocate." Chen and Mathews sat near me.

"Let's begin," Hollenbeck said, and read the accusations against Cole. "Excessive use of force during a unit shakedown in July," she said, and read the details about that chaotic day: a sudden search for a shank, Mathews's tussle with Cole, his emergency medication shot. Then she turned the proceeding over to Chen. Mathews sat quietly as his advocate gave the specific date and time of the shakedown and the events that led up to him receiving an injection of emergency medication.

"We're not contending that the shot was unwarranted," Chen

said, "but that during the events prior to it, Mr. Mathews was treated by Officer Cole in an unnecessarily harsh manner."

She lifted Mathews's chart from the table, opened it to a marked section, and read a note from that day: "'I heard punches being thrown and furniture breaking.'" It had been authored by Larsen. "Mr. Mathews never stated that he would not take the medication voluntarily," she'd added.

"I felt Officer Cole behaved in a reckless and cavalier manner," Larsen said when Hollenbeck asked for an explanation. "He was unduly rough. Everyone heard the violence, the smashing furniture. Mr. Mathews could easily have been seriously injured."

Cole shifted in his seat and shook his head. I watched Larsen. Her eyes stayed on Hollenbeck.

Lipscomb led Cole through his rebuttal. "Mr. Mathews is a tough customer," Cole said. "Each time I've come on Unit C, it's an emergency. That day we needed to search his room. He wouldn't comply. If I hadn't intervened decisively, another patient or staff member might have gotten hurt."

Then Hollenbeck called my name.

I knew Cole had been rough. I understood why Larsen might write him up. Still, our patients were difficult and dangerous. And to be frank, all else aside, I'd always been glad to see Cole walk onto the unit.

"Given Mr. Mathews's repeated episodes of violent and dangerous behavior," I said at my turn, "during the shakedown I believe Officer Cole operated within proper guidelines." I sat back and added Mathews to my growing list of patients to keep an eye on.

Mathews gave his side of the story—"I wasn't doing anything. He just attacked me."—then each representative summed up. Hollenbeck thanked everyone for attending.

"Officer Cole, you and Mr. Mathews will be contacted with the results of this inquiry," Hollenbeck said, and turned to the rest of us. "Nothing said here will leave this room."

OVER DINNER, INGRID broke the news that a Realtor had called about a house that seemed promising. "Last time we spoke, honey," Ingrid said evenly, "you'd committed to staying at Gomorrah. Has that changed?" Ingrid and John looked at me. "I'd understand either way," Ingrid said.

"Your job's not safe, Dad," John said. "We'll find a house later. Or move somewhere else."

I wondered if my job at Gomorrah hadn't forced John, at all of fourteen, to be too mature.

"If we moved," I said, "you'd have to change schools again."

"There are lots of schools," John said.

"You can't leave your practice," I said to Ingrid.

"We'll talk about that later," Ingrid said. "This is your time."

I was oddly frozen. I wanted to say: "You're right—my job is terrible. I'm going to get killed. Sorry about the house." But I didn't. Nor did I say: "Of course, I'll be fine. Let's do it." I didn't say anything. Then the dogs walked in.

"What do you think, Mulder?" I said. "Scully?" They both looked at me quizzically.

The house decision had always been theoretical; I'd never been faced with an actual house. Our future hinged on my job, but it was difficult to think straight. My feelings about Gomorrah changed, it seemed, by the day. I said I would stay. I said I would go.

John was right; Gomorrah wasn't safe. People there got hurt and hurt badly. I'd accumulated a list of patients on Unit C who wished me harm. And they had the means to do it.

But there was also Mr. Caruthers, NPR-man, the spangled shamanistic trick phone and watercolor I'd received at Christmas. Then there was the staff. What would I say to them? Or more accurately, what would I say to myself? That one I couldn't answer.

"Tell me a little about the house," I said finally.

"Are you sure?" Ingrid asked.

"No. But tell me anyway."

The following weekend we went to see the house, and within two weeks we'd made a final offer.

That night, I stopped in John's doorway. It was late and I was tired. Engrossed at his desk, he didn't see me.

For Christmas one year, Ingrid's parents had given John a complete set of *Star Wars* figures, which he always kept on a bookshelf. Now I noticed he'd set them carefully on the side of his desk nearest the window in a shrine-like semicircle around a small plastic fire pit, upon which he'd propped the 1959 Sandy Koufax baseball card. Yoda, Princess Leia, Luke, Darth Vader, and Obi-Wan Kenobi formed an inner ring while a host of Jedi warriors buffered them. Everyone facing out, lightsabers at the ready, they watched the rain-filled night.

"What you got there?" I asked.

John turned, and I gestured toward the setup. "It's like a protection ring," he said. "To ward off evil."

"Do you think you need protection?" I asked.

"It's not for me," John said. "It's for you."

CHAPTER TWENTY-ONE

You people would convict a grilled cheese sandwich of murder and the people wouldn't question it.

–Charles Manson

After two weeks, the rain stopped. So complete had been our soaking, however, that even on Friday, my tires still produced rooster tails from road pools. A flotilla of tow trucks continued to pull stranded cars out of encasing side-road mud. And near our home, a family of ducks nested on the median strip.

But the hospital was dry. Large, whistling fans blew like jet engines all week down the hallways. A barrage of towels, mops, and Lysol had eradicated the mold and moisture. The sally port disassembled its improvised bridge.

By Friday even the smell in the hallway had abated somewhat. I met Cohen outside our offices and he crinkled his nose. We headed to Unit C. Cohen went in first. I locked the door and had walked halfway to the nurses' station when McCoy appeared but slid right by me. I took a few more steps, then turned at the sound of keys hitting the main door lock. McCoy stood sentry-like just inside.

Carstairs stepped in, and McCoy's hand brushed her arm. This was bad. McCoy and I hadn't spoken much since the team meeting after he returned from court. I knew he was still mad, but I ran up to intervene. There was a momentary standoff. McCoy leveled his gaze and didn't give way.

"Mr. McCoy," Xiang finally said from behind me. "We have spoken about this."

"You bet, Mr. Xiang," McCoy said, and grudgingly stepped aside, then walked back down the hall and into his room.

Rounds over, Cohen and I stood. Before leaving the conference room, I gave him a quick update on the McCoy-Carstairs situation. Carstairs, still seated, spoke with Larsen.

"Can we talk a minute?" I said when she and Larsen had finished.

"Sure," Carstairs replied.

"Maybe you could join us for lunch?" I said. "Do you know the taco truck? The weather's fairly nice today. Bring a jacket. We can sit outside."

"Am I in trouble?"

"We just want to talk," Cohen said. "Maybe get to know each other a little better."

At twelve thirty, just off hospital grounds, our trio stood in line behind five Gomorrah nurses waiting to order the best Mexican food in town from the vending truck parked next to the sidewalk.

"That smells so good," Carstairs said when the man finally handed down our bags of food. "Is this truck always here?"

"Every day," Cohen said.

"I'm really glad I didn't know about it before," Carstairs said, and smiled.

We walked back across a big stretch of lawn and took seats at our regular metal picnic table under a spreading oak tree outside the fence. As we sat, a distant alarm rang and Carstairs winced.

"Will I ever get used to that sound?" she sighed, and set down her food.

"I don't know, but I haven't," I said.

We opened our bags, unwrapped burritos, and took a few bites. The alarm stopped and Carstairs relaxed noticeably. I felt better as well.

"Emily, do you plan to stay here at Gomorrah?" Cohen asked.

"We sure need the money," Carstairs said.

"You and your husband?" Cohen asked.

"I'm not married," Carstairs said. "I mean, I was. But a roadside bomb in Kandahar, Afghanistan, took care of that."

"I'm sorry for asking," Cohen said. "Forgive me."

"It was five years ago," Carstairs said. "For the first while, for the first long while, I didn't know if I could go on." She took a breath. "If it hadn't been for our son and me going back to school, who knows?"

"How old is your boy?" I asked, and Carstairs brightened.

"Jeremy is six," she said. "He was just a year old when Greg's Guard unit got the call. What about you?" Carstairs said, looking up. "Do you have kids?"

As we ate, we talked about John and Ingrid.

"Are you married, Dr. Cohen?" Carstairs asked.

"My girlfriend's an attorney," Cohen said. "Right now she's on the fence. But I'm getting ready to make my closing argument."

"Good luck," Carstairs said.

"What are your plans, Emily?" Cohen asked.

"I just want to give Jeremy a safe home that he can trust," she said. "Where people don't go away and never come back."

We folded our food wrappers into the paper bags. "We need to talk about Mr. McCoy," I said.

"I've been warned," Carstairs replied defensively.

"We know," Cohen added, "but we want to talk about him again."

Carstairs sat up straight. "Okay, talk," she said.

"What do you know about Mr. McCoy?" Cohen asked.

"I know he committed crimes," Carstairs said.

"McCoy has killed three men, probably four," I began. "He clubbed a Unit C patient, Mr. Wilkins, on the head with a chair. The man's brains oozed out of his head. And McCoy laughed."

Carstairs stared toward the horizon, then at me and Cohen. Tears lined her eyes.

"When I allow Mr. McCoy to walk me from the door to the nurses' station, everyone else leaves me alone," she said. "The hallway is empty. Haven't you noticed? Do you understand how important that is? I'm not stupid. I know McCoy is repugnant and that he's a killer. But it's a risk I'm willing to take." Carstairs pushed back her hair and went on. "Gomorrah is a jungle. I've read the patients' charts. Most of these guys are locked up for violent crimes against women. Don't you think I see how they look at me?" she continued. "I didn't know what Gomorrah was like before I came here. But I know what it's like now. Being safe is paramount; it's everything. How can you understand what it's like for a woman in there? Ask your female nurses. See what they tell you."

Carstairs leaned in slightly. "The nurses don't complain about the violence," she said angrily, "because they might lose their job.

I've heard them talk. If they lose their job, they lose their house. So they've made a trade as well. That's why they take the chance of getting hit. We all make trades. I'm willing to bet you guys do, too."

Carstairs took a breath. "And that's why I let McCoy walk beside me," she stated. "What am I supposed to do? Have Jeremy lose another parent?" Emotion heavy in her voice, she sighed. "Can you keep me safe?"

Carstairs collected her bag, stood, and walked away.

JANUARY ROLLED INTO February. The days were short. In the mornings, as I drove to work, frost tinged the roads and trees.

It was Friday and Nurse Hancock was retiring. Cohen and I were watching out a hallway window as what looked like the Macy's Thanksgiving Day Parade headed to Unit C. I'd never seen so many people on the hospital grounds. Nurses, techs, social workers, rehab therapists, doctors, maintenance people, administrators, and cops all carried covered dishes or lugged six-packs of soda.

We propped the front door open, and upon large tables in the main assembly room, a sea of food slowly accumulated. At Gomorrah, with such a culturally diverse staff, the food was routinely exotic and delicious. Hancock made some modest remarks and told a few touching stories about her three decades at Gomorrah. Dry eyes were few.

"Thank you for the friendship, support, and help you've given me over the years," Hancock said in conclusion. "May God bless all who live and work within these walls." She sat to thunderous applause.

After Hancock greeted an army of well-wishers, I caught her alone for a moment. "So, is it the beach with a good book?" I asked.

"The girls are done with college," Hancock said. "And after this shoulder thing is over, my husband and I plan to spend some time together. We're going to open a mission school near Zamboanga in the southern Philippines."

"That's Muslim insurgency country," I said. "You managed to pick the one place more dangerous than here."

"Where could I be needed more?"

"You're an amazing person," I said. "But you know that. Who will ever care as much for these patients as you do?"

"You all care as much as I do," Hancock said. "You just don't admit it."

I thought about that comment for a while. For more than a while.

At home that night, after John had gone to bed, I broke the cardinal rule and talked about my job.

"How was your day?" Ingrid asked. We sat on opposite ends of the sofa.

"A really good nurse retired today," I said. "Virginia Hancock. I told you about her."

"She's the one who called working at Gomorrah a Jesus job, right?"

"That's her."

"What made her so good?" Ingrid asked, and for the next hour we talked, really talked, for the first time in months. After a while, I mentioned how difficult it was passing patients in the hallways outside the unit. This struck a nerve.

"It seems to me," Ingrid said, "that the whole concept of Gomorrah is wrong. If it's a hospital and the patients are sick, then why the big fence and locked units? And if it's a prison, why the softball games, jogging groups, and open rooms?" Ingrid continued. "Walking to and from lunch is fine. But why do you have to be there? How can you rub shoulders with killers?"

Then Ingrid reiterated the most common question I get about Gomorrah. "Tell me again, why aren't there any guards?"

CHAPTER TWENTY-TWO

Disease, insanity, and death were the angels that attended my cradle, and since then have followed me throughout my life.

—Edvard Munch

Both on Unit C and in my life, events started to come to a head. One went well; the other didn't.

Late Wednesday afternoon I got a text from Ingrid. "Offer accepted," it said. "See you tonight."

I leaned back in my office chair. Then an alarm went off.

I ran ahead of Cohen, unlocked the door to Unit C, and followed a crowd to the nurses' station.

"I warned you," Xiang yelled, and kicked at Gomez, who lay on the ground covered by staff. Cohen restrained Xiang but only just.

"I'll stab the motherfucker," Cervantes screamed, and his ear flags shook. Three nurses had him pinned to a hallway wall. As they writhed, a sharpened metal eyeglass stem clinked to the ground.

Ten paces down a side hallway, a clutch of others consoled Hong, who wailed at the top of his lungs in Chinese. Unit B people formed a human perimeter and turned back the other patients who rushed up. I joined Cohen.

"Mr. Xiang," I said, "calm down."

Wild-eyed, Xiang sputtered in Vietnamese, then made one final lunge toward Gomez. Cohen grabbed Xiang's arm and yanked back, his elbow smacking me in the face and knocking me down.

From the ground, I saw the unit door open and a squad of cops' feet run down the hallway.

IN THE NURSES' station I held an ice pack to my face. Cohen looked stricken. "I'm so sorry," he said, and winced when I lowered my hand. I checked the mirror above the sink; a ring of purple grew around my right eye.

"It couldn't be helped," I said, and we went out to speak with the police.

Lieutenant Harrison took statements from the staff. "Gomez attacked Hong," Palanqui said. "In the middle of the hall. In broad daylight. He grabbed him from behind and pulled off his pants.

"Hong screamed," she continued. "That brought Cervantes, and the fight started."

"I pulled the alarm," Monabong added, and the remainder of the story was told.

"Is Hong okay?" Harrison asked, wrapping up.

"He's getting a rape test at County General Emergency," Palanqui replied.

"If there was any penetration," Kate Henry stated, "charges will be filed."

I'd learned that at Gomorrah it's possible to "pick up" charges if you commit a crime. They often get filed, but rarely does anything happen. And it's easy to understand why that is. A patient who commits an assault at Gomorrah came to Gomorrah because they'd already been judged incompetent for a previous crime. So they're usually found incompetent again. And they're sent back to Gomorrah for more treatment. Usually to the same ward. And even the same bed. We'd seen it when McCoy battered Wilkins. Gomorrah saw it a thousand times every year. Inside the fence, it was a Free Assault Zone.

"And Xiang?" Harrison asked.

"He went home," Cohen said. "I've never seen anybody so mad."

Lieutenant Harrison looked at me. "You okay, Doc?"

"Hey, I can take an elbow from a psychologist," I said.

"Get a doctor to look at that," Kate Henry said.

"I will."

And Ingrid did look at it. "Jesus, what now?" she said as I came in the door. I told her the unvarnished truth.

"Ben Cohen hit me with his elbow," I said. "It was an accident."

"You got elbowed in the face by your psychologist?" Ingrid asked. "That must be some story."

"I'll tell you at dinner," I said, and summoned a big smile. "But first, let's talk about the house."

"Dad, you look like Rocky," John said, walking out of his room. "Are you okay?"

"I'm fine, really," I said. "Let's eat."

The house was the big dinner topic. "They accepted our offer," Ingrid said. "Without a counter. We sign papers on Friday. I said you could be at the title company by five thirty."

"Not a problem," I said. "I'm really excited. Tell me about the plans for your bedroom," I said to John, and the rest of the conversation that evening was upbeat and happy.

Ingrid gave my eye a proper look before we retired. "Follow my finger," she said, and I did. She delicately probed the rim of my eye socket, feeling for the sort of damage Mathews had inflicted on Luella. She checked for blood behind the cornea. "Looks good," she concluded, her exam at an end.

Ingrid didn't know what else to say, nor did I. First stitches, now the shiner. We crawled into bed.

"It really was Cohen's elbow that hit me," I said.

"Boys will be boys," Ingrid replied.

I LEFT WORK early on Friday and drove to meet Ingrid at the title company office. The eye makeup Ingrid had applied that morning had worn off. She pulled a tube of foundation from her purse and did a quick touch-up before we entered the office. Inside, she explained to our Realtor and the escrow officers that I'd been hit by a door, which seemed to satisfy everyone. Then we signed stacks of papers and were congratulated on our new home. It was an exciting moment for us, becoming home owners again. Ingrid shone. I felt a little faint.

We'd been trapped with a mortgage before and had only recently escaped. And if a repeat of that problem was to be avoided, I needed a job. And for now, a job meant Gomorrah. I tried to put that out of my mind.

Afterward, Ingrid and I stood outside on the sidewalk. "I didn't think you were going to make it," she said, and gently touched my darkened eye. "Are you certain you aren't hurt worse than you think? I'm going to make you an appointment with the doctor."

"I got a little shaky," I said. "But it passed. I feel fine." I hugged her. "Congratulations, Dr. Home Owner," I said. "It's been a long haul."

Ingrid held me at arm's length. "I'm very happy."

ON MONDAY, XIANG didn't show up for work. Nor did he appear all the rest of that week. As was the custom at Gomorrah, everyone spoke about Xiang's absence obliquely. Then we soldiered on. Kate Henry ran rounds, and the following week, still with no word from Xiang, she introduced a new nurse.

"This is Bernice Hopkins," Kate Henry said at the beginning of rounds the first week in March. "She's filling in until Mr. Xiang returns."

"Have you worked at a state hospital before, Bernice?" Palanqui asked.

"No, dear, I haven't," Hopkins said. "I spent thirty years at a private psychiatric outpatient clinic. We treated children."

"How did you hear about this place?" Monabong inquired.

"The agency sent me over," Hopkins said. "I work for them part-time. I found retirement boring."

"You won't find this place boring," Cohen said.

"I hope not," replied Hopkins. She was an older white woman with a pleasant smile.

A round of introductions followed.

"Good Lord, what happened to your eye?" Hopkins said at my turn. The purple had morphed to green.

"Dr. Cohen hit me," I said. "It was an accident."

"I see," Hopkins said and gave Cohen a quick once-over.

After only a few days, it became apparent that Hopkins was in over her head. After two weeks, the situation had become untenable.

"Any word on Mr. Xiang?" I asked after rounds in mid-March. Hopkins wasn't at the conference room table. As had become her custom, she'd fled back to the nurses' station before the last patient's name was read.

"No one has heard anything," Kate Henry said. At Gomorrah, information about staff on leave was extremely difficult to obtain.

The rest of the staff shook their heads, then we turned to the matter at hand.

"Bernice is a sweet woman," Cohen said. "But this just isn't working out. She won't come to alarms."

"She's afraid to talk to the patients," Palanqui said. "She never leaves the nurses' station. Mr. Burns banged on the window yesterday and Hopkins hid in the med room. She was crying."

The situation boiled over the following week.

At rounds on Tuesday, Hopkins seemed unusually calm. She stayed for the entire meeting. "If there's anything you need," she said as I stood, "please ask."

"Thanks," I said. "I will."

Kate Henry stopped me in the hall. "Hopkins seems to be getting used to the place," she said. "Maybe she's feeling better."

Hopkins's improved mood persisted for the next two days. By Thursday, she was downright cheerful. "Have a great day," she said, beaming to the staff after rounds.

That afternoon an alarm rang. I ran from my office. The Unit B people flew down, and everyone rushed onto the unit.

Near the nurses' station, Ortega lay on the ground, his wheelchair overturned against a wall. Above him, Caruthers, his roommate, and Mathews had squared off. Mathews taunted and danced. Caruthers stood quiet and ready. Bravely, two nurses scuttled between the combatants, hastily grabbed Ortega under the arms, and dragged him to safety.

"You slapped a sick old man," Caruthers said, and edged right. "He's in a wheelchair. I'm not. Why don't you slap me?" Caruthers towered over Mathews.

"Fuck you," Mathews said. "You want a part of me? Come get it." Mathews slammed both fists on his chest and edged left.

The staff and I stood in a circle, ready to jump in.

As Mathews and Caruthers continued to taunt, I glanced into the nurses' station. Hopkins rummaged through her purse and extracted a small brown prescription bottle, twisted off the cap, calmly tapped two pills into her palm, and downed them. She bent and took a quick swig from the station sink tap. Straightening her smock, she wobbled slightly and stepped forward.

Hopkins swung the station door open, marched out, and stood directly in front of Mathews. "Knock this shit off," she said. "I've had enough of your foolishness. Do you hear me?" She wagged a finger.

"Get the fuck out of the way," Mathews said, and tried to brush Hopkins aside. But Hopkins pushed back.

"This has to stop," she shouted. "I won't be scared anymore. Do you hear me?" Hopkins's face grew red. She trembled. "I said, do you hear me?" Behind us the cops pushed through the unit door and ran down the hall.

Mathews flicked a glance at the approaching police and it was over. "Yes, ma'am, I hear you," Mathews said, and stood down.

"Good." Hopkins huffed triumphantly, turned, and swayed away. Randy caught her from behind, bracing her by the elbows.

"You'll never be scared like this again, Miss Bernice," Randy said, and started walking toward the exit door. "I promise."

Caruthers gently collected Ortega off the ground and set him back in his wheelchair. Ortega patted both arms and both legs and touched his face. "*Estoy bien, gracias a dios*," he said.

Mathews turned to Caruthers. "Sorry for the disrespect, man," he said. "Are we cool?"

Caruthers nodded. "We're cool."

Randy and Hopkins stopped at the unit door. "You don't ever have to come back," Randy said, and undid the lock.

"Thank you, Jesus," Hopkins sighed, and slumped onto Randy's shoulder.

CHAPTER TWENTY-THREE

The rain goes pitter
The blood patter
With a thud of metal the razor falls.
—from "The Tale of Shadow DeHart" by A Blissful Dirge

The next Monday, Xiang came back. When Cohen and I walked onto the unit, he stepped out of the nurses' station and said, "Rounds. You're almost late." Then he pointed to the faint remnant of my shiner. "Your eye better?" he asked.

"It's fine," I replied.

We followed Xiang and sat with the assembled staff in the conference room, smiles all around the table. Kate Henry shrugged.

"Mr. Boudreaux," Xiang began, and opened his big black binder, "had a good night. Slept well." He went through each patient, not missing a beat. The staff made their usual comments. I wrote my daily to-do list on the back of an envelope.

"Welcome back, Mr. Xiang," I said at the end of rounds, and everyone chimed in similarly.

"Thank you," Xiang replied, and gathered up his black book. "Glad to be here." Then he walked out of the room.

"Do we know what happened?" I asked Kate Henry.

"I came to work and he was here," she said.

"Thank God for that," Cohen said.

"Amen," more than one person added, and the staff headed for the door.

"Don't leave, you two," Palanqui said and motioned to Cohen and me. "Spring is here and you know what that means?"

"The patients dance around the maypole?" Cohen asked, and we sat back down.

"No maypole," Palanqui said. "March Madness. Spring is basketball season. Our team here and the one up on Unit B need coaches. We thought you guys would be perfect."

Cohen's wheels began to turn. "I'll take the crew from Unit B," he said. "Mike Morgan may be a wheeler-dealer, but I think he can play ball. We'll clean the floor with you flat-landers down here."

I smiled. "It sounds fun."

"The gym is free for practice Tuesday and Thursday afternoons starting next week," Palanqui said. "There'll be four teams in all, with a championship contest at the end."

"I'll take Thursday," Cohen said.

"Tuesday works for me."

"The first game is a week from Friday," Palanqui added. "You'll play each other."

"That's a win for us," Cohen said smugly.

"In your dreams," I countered, but I knew Cohen was right; Unit C had nobody.

Leaving the ward, Cohen and I passed Xiang standing at the end of the hallway. He was speaking with two patients. They talked and he listened.

"I won't see you for a bit," I said to Cohen when we reached our offices.

"Vacation?" Cohen said.

"We bought a new home," I said. "We'll be moving next week."

"Moving is always a joy," Cohen said with a grin.

"It beats being here," I said.

"BACK TO THE salt mines," I lamented to Ingrid and John when I left the following Tuesday morning. As I told Cohen, we'd spent the last week moving into our new home, and I did welcome the break from Unit C.

"Be careful," Ingrid said, and sent me off with a hug.

My drive, ten minutes longer than before, wasn't a problem. I watched the sun rise and listened to an extra NPR news segment.

After rounds, I pulled a yellow sheet of legal paper from my shirt pocket and quickly jotted down some names. Cohen glanced over my shoulder. "Your team?" he asked.

"What do you think?" I said, and tipped the paper toward him.

"The trophy is mine," he said. "While you were moving, we've been practicing."

In the nurses' station, I clicked on the intercom, called the seven names from my sheet of paper, and asked them to gather near the station door. In three minutes, Floyd Traylor, Vernon Chambers, Caruthers, NPR-man, Leon Smith, Shawn Carver, and Boudreaux all formed up and looked about warily.

"I have something I think you'll like," I said, and walked out the door, list in hand.

"No more baseball," Carver said.

"Baseball Tonight," NPR-man blurted. "After that the traffic news."

"When's lunch?" Traylor asked.

"Give the man a chance," Caruthers said. "What's going on, Doc?"

I held up my list. "It's hospital basketball season," I said. "We need to field a team. I picked you guys. What do you think?"

Everyone looked around. "I think you're nuts," Chambers said.

Monabong walked up. "We've been challenged by Unit B," she said. "We can't lose to them."

The men murmured.

"This will get you off the unit for a few hours each week," Monabong continued, and this brought nearly unanimous assent. Only Boudreaux looked sullen. "Are you in?" I asked.

"Yeah, I guess," Boudreaux replied, and I saw a flash of the man from our first meeting.

"I have wicked basketball skills," NPR-man added, and everyone turned. "Also nunchuk skills, bo-staff skills, and computer-hacking skills."

No one was certain they'd heard right.

"That's wonderful, Michael," Monabong said finally. "You'll be a tremendous asset to the team."

"Girls only like guys with great skills," NPR-man said.

"That's right," Monabong said. "They certainly do."

Cohen and I had lunch together. "NPR-man stopped talking about NPR this morning," I said.

"His meds finally kick in?" Cohen asked.

"Something happened," I said. "He switched to *Napoleon Dynamite*."

The Unit C team met that afternoon on the basketball court. As we began to dribble and shoot, it became apparent that any initial enthusiasm I'd harbored had been seriously misplaced. Traylor bounced the ball three times, then threw it two feet over the top of the backboard. Smith did little better. An older man who'd apparently once possessed athletic skills, he stood at the free-throw line and shot the ball two-handed. It hit the bottom of the net.

"That's a good start," I said as I collected the ball and bounced it to Chambers, a tallish man I'd figured for a rebounder. As practice progressed, he did grab a few missed shots off the glass backboard and propelled the ball to one of our teammates. Caruthers had remnant talent and could clearly keep control of the ball. "Point guard," I said. The point guard is the squad general. He dribbles the ball up the court and distributes it. We looked to be okay there.

I'd taken NPR-man because of his age. Bouncing around the unit all day, he clearly had stamina. I threw him the ball. He held it up. "How much you want to bet I can throw a football over them mountains?" he said, then hurled the ball toward the sidewall and took off running down the court.

"Good hustle," I shouted. I retrieved the ball and flipped it to Boudreaux.

Boudreaux spun the ball in front of him and it skipped back into his hands. He cradled it above his head, bent both knees, and sent the orb in a perfect arc directly through the hoop. The ball made that magic sound described as "nothing but net." He'd made a twenty-five-foot shot.

I bounced the ball to Boudreaux again. He took a step back and smoothly drained a second long jump shot. We stared in awe, except for NPR-man, who ran back and forth underneath the opposite basket. "I caught you a delicious bass. I caught you a delicious bass," he called out repeatedly.

"You played ball," I said, and threw the ball back toward Boudreaux.

"A little," he replied, and took off, grabbed the ball in midstride, reversed himself under the basket, and banked the pill into the hoop left-handed.

My mind raced. Realistic thoughts of the championship trophy reappeared. Captivated by Boudreaux, we continued to watch in wonder as he moved gracefully, repeatedly dropping the ball neatly into the basket. That's why it took a while for us to notice that NPR-man had stopped talking. We heard a crash and turned. NPR-man's head bounced off the hardwood floor. His body went rigid, then, beginning with one arm and spreading across his body, he started seizing.

I hit my alarm and ran to NPR-man's side. The main job for a medical person during a seizure is to prevent someone else from jamming their fingers into the stricken person's mouth so they won't "swallow their tongue." No one swallows their tongue, but people do get bitten. I kept everyone away and made certain NPR-man didn't injure himself further.

Inside of two minutes, the gym doors burst open and ample help arrived. Bangban escorted my team back to the unit. As they left, a paramedic crew ran in, and, with their attention, NPR-man's seizure stopped. Intravenous line running, the medics got NPR-man on a gurney and rolled off.

Cohen burst in the far door. "What happened?" he asked, and pulled for breath.

"NPR-man had a seizure," I said.

"That's terrible," Cohen said. "Is he okay?"

"I'll call the ER when I get back to the office," I said. "They'll need to run some tests."

A full-blown seizure in someone without epilepsy is usually caused by only a few conditions: low blood sugar, substance withdrawal, or something bad like an infection in your brain, a burst blood vessel, or a tumor.

The last to leave, I locked the basketball in a cabinet. Cohen and I headed back to the unit.

The nurses' station was crowded. Standing with Xiang, the day staff, and the cops was Dr. Francis. She'd come with a man in a suit. This wasn't good. Suits at Gomorrah always meant trouble.

"Michael Tomlin had a seizure," I said, hoping that was the source of the commotion.

"We heard," Xiang said. "I called the County ER; he's having a CT scan now. But that's just one problem."

"The extension letter you wrote for Raymond Gomez," Dr. Francis said, "somehow got delayed in transit and arrived at court a week late. By then his legal hold had expired." She held up two official-looking papers. "The public defender challenged the legality of extending an expired hold and the judge upheld the motion. He ordered Gomez released immediately."

"That can't be," Cohen said. "He just tried to rape Hong. There must be some mistake."

Dr. Francis introduced the suit. "This is Mitchell Lin, from hospital legal."

"We filed an emergency appeal," Lin, a slim Asian man, said. "We should hear back within the hour. If the judge doesn't reverse," Lin added, "hospital police will escort Gomez out through the sally port."

Xiang became visibly upset. "This isn't right," he said. "What can that judge be thinking?"

"There are lots of judges from lots of counties," Dr. Francis said. "Most are very good. But a few have a different understanding about what goes on here. I think they've seen *Cuckoo's Nest* one too many times."

It was true. I'd seen strange things happen in court. During my training, a judge had released a mentally crippled schizophrenic man from the LA County hospital to live underneath a car and eat garbage from a Dumpster. This was the man's plan for food, clothing, and shelter, the legal bar for hospital release. And despite our strenuous objections, the judge concurred.

"I know Judge Bates," Lin said. "You better start collecting the patient's things."

Lin was right. Gomez did leave. In short order we got the fax confirming his release. He packed up his things and said, "Fuck my family," when asked if he wanted them called.

"I told you I was being railroaded," he shouted to the assembled patients, who had immediately gotten wind of the discharge. "Don't let these assholes fuck with you."

Cohen asked if Gomez's victims should be notified and was told by Lin that unless a specific person had been threatened, nothing could be done. He claimed that since Gomez had been officially discharged, it would be a "privacy invasion" to interfere.

Gomez told me where I could stick them when I offered him prescriptions for his medications. Duffel bag slung over one shoulder, he accepted the general acclaim of the ward patients, and then—Lin, Dr. Francis, and Kate Henry in tow—he was escorted out the door.

All afternoon the patients continued to hum. McCoy summed

up the general feeling. "That son of a bitch beat the hangman and they still let him go," he said. "I'm next, I know it."

Rounds went long the following morning. After discussing the patients, we spoke about Gomez.

"These things happen," Kate Henry said.

"He's going to rape another woman," Monabong said angrily. "Then you should ask her how she feels about 'these things' happening."

"In our country," Palanqui said, "Mr. Gomez would have been dead a long time ago."

"What kind of fucked-up deal is this?" Cohen asked, repeating a variation of Ingrid's reaction from the night before, and mine as well.

Only Xiang remained silent. "Mr. Xiang," Cohen said, "what do you think about all this?"

Xiang collected his black book and left the room. I didn't like the look in his eyes.

At three thirty, the end of the nursing shift, I waited outside Unit C. All the nurses filed out, but Xiang wasn't with them.

"Where's Mr. Xiang?" I asked Monabong.

"He went home early," she said.

After work I drove to Xiang's house.

I'd given him a lift home once last summer when he had car trouble. After a few wrong turns, I recognized a small flutter of Buddhist prayer flags tethered to a traditional Asian bamboo porch rail. Xiang's car sat in the drive.

When no one answered the door, I walked around the side of the house and found him sitting alone on the rear cement deck. He wore a thin white robe over his work clothes and was placing pieces of paper into a small fire.

Xiang nodded me over and I sat on the cement as well.

"Will you do my family a great honor," Xiang said, "and put ghost money into the fire?"

He passed me a thin sheet of paper, which had a gold stamp and "$5,000,000,000" printed on it. I dropped it into the tiny blaze. Xiang followed with another. We alternated like this until an entire stack of the money disappeared into the dark smoke.

"For my mother," Xiang said and didn't look up. "It's called ghost money or heaven money," he continued in a quiet, deliberate tone. "We send it so she can buy all the things she didn't have here." Xiang dropped more bills into the fire and fanned the flames with his hand.

"My mother died when I was young," he said. "During the American war in Vietnam. My father was killed by Vietcong. My mother raised my brother and me alone. She worked day and night. One day, she worked in the rice field. Two American soldiers found her and raped her. 'Gook,' they called her. They thought no one saw them. But I saw. My mother was never the same. She died the next year."

My older brother lost a leg in Vietnam. My youth basketball coach was killed by friendly fire. I had emotion attached to that country, as well. In silence, we put another stack of gold-tinted bills into the small inferno.

"I owe you an apology," Xiang said. "I behaved very badly when Mr. Gomez attempted to rape Hong. Please forgive me."

Xiang continued, "When I was gone from the hospital, I flew back to Vietnam to see that rice field one more time. I thought if I saw it, maybe I could be done with that place once and for all." He smiled sadly. "But I learned you can never really be done with some things."

Xiang stared ahead as the money fire dimmed. "I came to this country as a teenager," he said. "I love this country. It gave me my education, my wife, and my children. It gave me everything I have. But I don't understand this country. I don't understand the American soldiers. I don't understand why they raped my mother when she was innocent. And I don't understand the American courts. Why they set Gomez free when he is guilty."

Xiang stood. "You came here today," he said. "Because you were concerned about me. For this, I am grateful."

I stood as well. Words wouldn't come. "I'll see you tomorrow," I said at last.

Xiang looked at his watch. "My kids will be home soon," he said. "They were born here. Like their mother, they are Americans. I don't understand them too much, either."

CHAPTER TWENTY-FOUR

Much Madness is divinest Sense–
To a discerning Eye–
Much sense–the starkest Madness–
'Tis the Majority
In this, as All, prevail–
Assent–and you are sane–
Demur–you're straightway dangerous–
And handled with a Chain–

–Emily Dickinson, "Much Madness Is Divinest Sense" (620)

Driving home, I'd tried to sort through my feelings about the afternoon episode with Xiang. He was much more than just a nurse. He felt like a friend, family even. I felt the same way about many of the staff on Unit C. Facing shared adversity, we'd bonded. We had each other's backs. We functioned as a team in the real sense of the word. Each person had a job, and they did it despite great odds. And Xiang was the captain. I don't recall admiring anyone more.

As a member of the Unit C team, I didn't feel so adrift anymore. I wasn't comfortable—at Gomorrah, I don't think that's possible—but I felt less like a rookie. I'd come to some temporary peace with my job; the struggle seemed to have abated somewhat. I knew this could all be temporary. I knew that whatever truce I'd agreed to with Gomorrah could all be dashed in one alarm bell, one fist to a nurse's face. But following the AA mantra, those were problems for another day.

That day I reveled in the pleasure of our new home. It was open and spacious, but not pretentious. The backyard was fenced for the dogs. A raised-bed garden plot had been installed by the previous owners. Ingrid had a way with plants. I knew she had designs on that garden.

The evening was pleasant and calm. Just what I needed. For the first night in a dozen, I slept well. I didn't recall any dreams. The next morning, however, brought a waking nightmare.

"It's cancer," Dr. Singh, the internist from County General, said over the phone when I called after rounds on Tuesday. He was the doctor for Michael Tomlin, NPR-man. The general surmise among the staff had been that Tomlin might have seized from diabetes. "Or something simple like that," Palanqui said. But it was not to be. An MRI scan had revealed a tumor in Tomlin's right femur that had spread to his lungs and brain.

Singh said both radiation and chemotherapy were treatment options but that the cancer was fairly advanced. He gave Michael six months. He mentioned that with medication, Tomlin's seizures would eventually come under control and then there would be no need for further medical hospitalization. When Tomlin was ready, he said, he'd call back. Tomlin would be coming home.

"Is he a martial artist?" Singh asked before we hung up.

"NPR . . . I mean Mr. Tomlin? I don't think so."

"I was just curious," Singh said. "He speaks of nunchuck skills constantly."

I convened the staff in the conference room and gave them the grim report. Quiet tears were shed, but no one spoke.

"Goddamn it," Cohen finally said, and we left it at that.

I didn't know if we should cancel the basketball game that Friday, but we didn't. And I was glad. Being in the gym had a good effect on me. The rhythmic bouncing of the ball. The constant motion. The attention needed to coach made everything else go away for a while.

With the loss of Tomlin, I was down to six players. But we soldiered on. After arriving in the gym, I unlocked a cabinet and produced two practice balls.

A few staff members and cops came to watch. We'd just said hello when the back gym door opened. Cohen and the Unit B team ran in. They were all clad in gold T-shirts with "Lakers" stenciled on the back.

Eight men in all, they scooped up the basketballs, formed two lines, and executed some well-rehearsed layup drills, then practiced shooting in an organized fashion. And Cohen had been right about Mike Morgan. Although in his early forties, he still could move well, and when he shot the ball, it ended up somewhere near the basket.

Mark Halston, a janitor from upstairs, appeared in a black-and-white striped referee shirt and blew his whistle. He had the game ball.

"Two ten-minute halves," he said. "I run the clock. Officer Bangban keeps the score." He pointed at one basket. "Unit B, that's your end. Unit C, the other."

"Unit B's ball. Let's go."

"Okay, guys," I said. "Game time."

Boudreaux sat out initially, to prolong the surprise. The remaining five took the court.

Halston handed the ball to a Unit B man, who threw it to a Laker teammate, and the contest was under way.

Procedural problems plagued the early going. Twice Chambers grabbed a missed shot and put it into the wrong basket. Small scuffles erupted and words were exchanged, something not entirely unexpected from ten men not predisposed to playing nicely with others.

Teamwork suffered. Despite my constant remonstrations to "pass it around," every man basically just grabbed the ball and shot it.

At halftime we trailed ten to six, but four of their points had been scored by Chambers. Still, Cohen looked confident. Morgan strutted out for the second half.

Boudreaux walked onto the court, and our plans changed. "Give the ball to Boudreaux," I said. It became my mantra from then on.

Boudreaux put on a show. Fed by Caruthers, he drained shot after shot. And those he missed, he rebounded and smoothly put back in. I sat him down for the last two minutes of the game, and the circus returned. At the final whistle, Carver let fly a discus shot that slammed against the back wall ten feet above the backboard.

We won by twenty. I huddled with my team after the game and doled out congratulations. We put our hands together in the middle of a circle. "Let's win the championship for Michael Tomlin," I said, and everyone gave a hurrah.

"You won't lose a game," Cohen said as we walked back to the unit.

"I know," I replied.

"You never said you had Kobe Bryant," Cohen said.

And for the rest of the season, that's what we called Boudreaux.

• • •

MONDAY BROUGHT APRIL. During rounds, a scream erupted from a nearby hallway. We ran. Caruthers stood in the middle of the corridor. "Help! Help!" he shouted and waved. We picked through anxious patients to get to his room. When the staff rushed up, Caruthers, tears streaming down his cheeks, pointed inside.

On the bed nearest the window, Manuel Ortega lay still. I walked in. Ortega's eyes were fixed, his skin cold. I checked his neck; he had no pulse. I pulled the white bedsheet up over his face.

"Do something!" Caruthers implored from the doorway.

"Get everyone away, please," I said to Cohen, who cleared the crowd. Cohen closed the door behind Caruthers.

"Do something," Caruthers pled, and stepped forward, then pulled back. "Help him."

"He's gone, Tom," I said.

"No!" Caruthers wailed. "Do CPR. Call an ambulance . . . Do . . ." he sputtered, then began to openly sob.

I broke the boundary rule again. "I'm so sorry, Tom," I said as he wept on my shoulder.

Caruthers slowly regained control. He rubbed his face with his shirt. "Oh, no . . ." he moaned, and looked at Ortega.

"Let's go to a side room," I said.

"May I see him one more time?" Caruthers asked.

"Of course," I said, and we walked to the bedside. I pulled down the sheet and Caruthers drew in a breath. Caruthers touched Ortega's face, wiped a new tear off his own cheek, and bent down. He whispered something into Ortega's ear, and then he pulled the sheet back up and turned. "Let's go," he said.

A few patients patted Caruthers's arm. "Sorry, man," Smith said.

"We're here if you need us," Cohen added.

Caruthers nodded. We walked to the side room.

On the unit, two rooms had been dedicated for situations like this. They each contained a pair of upholstered chairs and a small table. I unlocked the door and we sat.

I waited for Caruthers to speak. "Manuel was a father to me," he said at last. "You remember my real father . . ." He caught himself and touched the side of his head.

Caruthers's father had killed his mother in front of Caruthers and his three sisters. He strangled her.

"I remember," I said.

At the time, Caruthers told me, his father, after killing his mother, had beaten the kids in a drunken rage. Before the police arrived, Caruthers's father hit his sister Marjorie in the face so hard that she lost an eye. Young Caruthers had attempted to defend his sister and, after a brief altercation, got thrown down the apartment stairs. Caruthers received a severely broken arm, but the doctors who operated on Marjorie said he probably saved his sister's life. She couldn't have survived another blow from her father.

For six months Caruthers came to his outpatient visits in an elaborate arm cast, signed on every square inch by schoolmates. When that cast was replaced some months later, I noted gang signs written on the plaster instead of well wishes.

Caruthers's mood had taken a nose dive when he had to testify at his father's murder trial. He'd been offered a pass, but he refused. "I wanted to see that asshole get what he deserved," he told me. Soon after, Caruthers was hospitalized with suicidal thoughts. I adjusted his medications and we spoke frequently. His only regret: "I wish I'd been big enough to kill my father," he'd said.

"Manuel made some of that better," Caruthers said. "He cared for me like a son."

We talked for an hour. "Are you going to be okay?" I asked. "You're not planning on hurting yourself?" Questions about suicide are best asked directly. Many people think they can generate dangerous feelings, but they actually reveal them.

"I'm okay," Caruthers said.

"If you start to feel bad," I said, "will you promise to speak with a staff person?"

"I promise," Caruthers said.

AS THE UNIT C basketball crew cruised through the regular schedule, more people began attending the games. We never came close to losing. The season was a clear sail on calm waters. Boudreaux was magnificent, and even Carver got in the swing and muscled in a few points.

Most of the Unit C staff lined the sidelines for our final regular-season contest. Again, Unit B was the opponent.

As game time approached, Cohen huddled with his golden team. He took Morgan aside and spoke to him strenuously. I tried to imagine what he was saying. Halston blew his whistle, assigned the baskets, and held out the ball to Unit B. "Let's go," he said.

"Game time," I said. It had become my lucky saying. The game began and went according to script. We led by twelve at halftime and by twenty-two near the end. With a minute left, Caruthers bounced the ball to Boudreaux, who performed his patented helicopter spin move and left-handed reverse scoop layup. Only this time, a player from Unit B stood in the way. Boudreaux mowed him down. Halston blew a whistle and raised his hand. Boudreaux completed the acrobatic play, the ball nestling gently into the hoop. He turned triumphantly.

"Foul," Halston said. "No basket. Charging. Unit B ball."

Boudreaux stood for a moment. His head ticked twice, his shoulders grew tight, and his visage hardened. "No goddamn way," he bellowed, and rushed Halston, who stepped back but didn't cave. Boudreaux glowered over him.

"I should shove that whistle down your goddamn, bloodsucking throat," Boudreaux snarled as both sidelines cleared and the staff ran up to shield Halston. The cops edged Boudreaux away.

"Season's over," Xiang said.

The other players formed up, waiting for an escort back to their units. Seemingly back under control, Boudreaux motioned toward me. "I'm sorry, Coach," he said. "I apologize. My behavior was totally unwarranted."

"You mean that?" I said.

"Yeah, Coach, I'm really sorry," Boudreaux said. "It won't happen again."

I called over Cohen and Xiang. The three of us approached Boudreaux, who repeated his apology. Then we moved to where Halston stood.

"I'm sorry, sir," Boudreaux said. "This is all my fault. It was a good call."

"Thanks," Halston said, but he still looked unnerved.

I waited a few seconds. "There's only the championship game

left," I said. "What do you think? It's not for two weeks. He'll be fine by then."

Everyone looked at one another. "Can you keep him under control?" Halston asked.

"I'll make certain he understands," I said. "No more trouble."

Another moment. "Okay," Halston said.

I'm ashamed to admit how relieved I was.

I caught Halston on his way out. "What do you hear about Tillson?" I asked, and thought back to doing CPR after the softball game.

"Hasn't been back," Halston said. "We never heard anything more."

I collected my team and we headed out of the gym. All the way to Unit C, Boudreaux and I—Kobe Bryant and Phil Jackson, star player and coach—confidently walked side by side.

I'd completely lost perspective, which in sports isn't uncommon. In retrospect, it was all easy to see. But in retrospect, everything is easy to see. My basketball squad did play one more game. And it nearly cost a life.

That night I closed my computer, locked the office, and left work. I passed Cohen in the hall heading in the other direction.

"Close call with Boudreaux today," Cohen said. "Good luck in the championship game."

"You too," I replied. "I think Boudreaux learned his lesson."

"I hope so," Cohen said. "He's one hell of a player."

I agreed. "And that's still one hell of a smell," Cohen added, and looked to the ceiling.

I'd been so distracted I hadn't noticed. We parted, he to his office and I to the main entrance.

As I walked to my truck, a police cruiser slowly eased out from a side drive and hovered just out of range. I got that familiar chill. As before, the car didn't pass, didn't gain or lose distance. I walked straight for the sally port.

Under the light from the exit, the cop car gently swung away. Alone, Detective Levin was driving. He touched a finger to the bill of his cap and eased back into the night.

I didn't stop to think until I was safely in my truck, the doors locked. I realized I'd never received any follow-up information on the report I'd given about the second cigarette sale. I'd never heard anything about a patient escape. And no patient had ever been reported missing.

CHAPTER TWENTY-FIVE

Madness does not always howl. Sometimes, it is the quiet voice at the end of the day saying, "Hey, is there room in your head for one more?"

–Despair, Inc.

That next Monday, Michael Tomlin came back to Unit C. What followed, for me, was a time for learning lessons.

"I have great nunchuck skills," Tomlin said as he was escorted onto the unit, one officer on either side ready to assist if Tomlin wobbled. He hadn't yet gotten the hang of the crutches he now needed to walk. Everyone crowded around, all truly delighted to see Tomlin again. I was surprised at the emotion his return generated. Hugs came from the nurses and not a few tears. The congregated patients let out a chorus of cheers and hearty hellos. It wasn't until some months later, after we'd heard of Tomlin's passing, that I realized how long he'd actually been a patient on Unit C. He'd come to the unit at age nineteen. He died having just turned thirty. And all those years, all the exuberance, all the energy, had been spent on Unit C.

Tomlin's return was particularly meaningful for Xiang. He had a special affinity for Tomlin and while never truly reciprocated, it never wavered. For the two weeks before Tomlin was transferred to a medical/psychiatric facility called the Meadows, fifty miles from Gomorrah, Xiang rarely left Tomlin's side.

On the day of his actual discharge, Xiang carefully packed Tomlin's things in two large duffel bags.

"I have great bo-staff skills," Tomlin said repeatedly as Xiang worked.

"Yes, you do, Michael," Xiang replied every time.

When Xiang finished, a crowd of patients had gathered outside Tomlin's room. Many men shook Tomlin's hand and wished him well. Caruthers gave him a hug. "Take care of that leg," Hong said. We hadn't told anyone about Tomlin's medical condition but they all knew. "God bless you," more than one person echoed.

"You come to New Orleans," Boudreaux said, "I'll put you up. We'll have a fine time."

"I caught you a delicious bass," Tomlin said.

"We'll fry that up real good, too," Boudreaux replied, and gently gripped Tomlin's arm.

The staff in turn bid Tomlin farewell. Cohen, Randy, and I shook his hand. The nurses all gave him a hug. Tears were shed. But not by Tomlin. "I have amazing bo-staff skills," he said, and broke out in a huge grin.

Xiang accompanied Tomlin and the police off the unit. I locked the door behind them. Through the small window, I saw Xiang stop and take Tomlin aside. He enfolded him in an embrace, then tilted Tomlin's head and kissed his forehead. Xiang turned and walked back to the unit.

The first lesson I learned was this: regardless of a person's crimes—Tomlin had bombed a school, killing children—if you live with them long enough, a relationship forms. I liked Michael Tomlin and was sad to see him leave. But upon reflection, those feelings were profoundly disturbing. Imagine the grief of Tomlin's victims. Imagine how different their farewells had been.

After Tomlin left, a second bed on Unit C came open. We heard that Mr. Wilkins, the man McCoy battered, would not be coming back. It wasn't unusual for Gomorrah to keep a patient's bed reserved when they left the unit for whatever reason: going to the medical hospital, court, or home. The general surmise among the staff was that Wilkins had finally died, but no one knew for sure. The next day, however, a nurse said her sister worked at the county hall of records and Wilkins's death certificate had come across her desk.

Wilkins's death brought up the issue of new charges against McCoy. It was spoken about at rounds but in that vague circular way that all such issues were discussed at Gomorrah. With McCoy having committed the crime last September and then recertified as incompetent the following December, it wasn't a stretch to conclude that if charged with Wilkins's murder, McCoy would be found incompetent to stand trial again.

This taught me another lesson. The news about Wilkins finally got me to understand why nobody talked about the violence at Gomorrah. It was the overwhelming impotence. We'd all witnessed McCoy's brutal assault. Yet we still lived with him. We knew he would never be punished. We also knew that in the future, there would be more violence. And that no one would ever be punished for those crimes, either. We would just have to get along with those violent people, as well.

Rocking the boat did no good and was even counterproductive. The folks in Sacramento didn't care, administration turned a deaf ear, and the assaulters just got mad. Then they might turn on you. The logical outcome of complaining about the violence at Gomorrah was more violence.

My final lesson was learned from the morning paper the day after Tomlin left the hospital. I'd flipped open the *Napa Valley Register* before leaving for work. "Child Killer Goes Free," the headline blared. "School Bomber Released from Napa State Hospital." Beneath this ran a picture of Tomlin taken years before at his original court hearing. His hair stood wild and uncombed. A menacing look on his face, he seemed poised to leap at the camera. A second photo, taken from ground level and looking up, showed the towering Gomorrah fence.

Ingrid wondered how such a release came to happen. I explained it was Michael Tomlin, the patient we used to call NPR-man. I told her that Tomlin had terminal bone cancer and it was a compassionate discharge, that his family didn't want him to die in a state mental hospital. She agreed that the cancer was a real shame and that the family's wishes were certainly reasonable. "But still," she concluded. "Kids . . . ?"

Even then, the lessons weren't quite done. The following week I learned a great deal about the production and consumption of alcohol.

The week had been quiet, always a blessing. After rounds on Thursday, however, Floyd Traylor, generally so mild mannered that even when his name was mentioned at rounds most staff members had difficulty recalling much about him, weaved unsteadily past the nurses' station window, then staggered as if stricken with palsy.

We rushed out into the hall. Before anyone could reach him, however, Traylor pantomimed someone inhaling deeply. "Smells like teen spirit!" he boomed, then convulsed in laughter, paused, and collapsed into a heap.

Palanqui activated her alarm. The staff gathered. I dropped to my knees and lifted Traylor's eyelids with a thumb. His pupils appeared normal, which ruled out, for the moment, a serious head event. I felt his neck for a pulse. That too seemed fine.

Palanqui produced a blood pressure cuff, and she expertly bound it around Traylor's arm and began to squeeze the rubber ball attachment. The cuff expanded; the ball wheezed. She listened inside his elbow with the bell of a stethoscope.

The unit door banged open and a clatter of feet pounded the hall tile. "It's medical," Monabong shouted, and the newly arrived Unit B people formed a human shield around Traylor, the nurses, and me.

"BP, one twenty over eighty-five," Palanqui said.

Monabong felt Traylor's wrist. "Pulse eighty-seven and steady. Do we call a code blue?" she asked.

"Wait," Palanqui replied as the air hissed out of her pressure cuff. She leaned over and put her face close to Traylor's, then gestured to Monabong, who did the same. They both sat back on their knees.

"He's drunk," Palanqui said. I leaned in and smelled his breath as well. It was alcohol.

I listened to Traylor's chest with the stethoscope. Heart and breathing sounded fine. "Let him sleep it off in the side room," I said. "Ms. Palanqui, stay with him. Any change, let me know."

The alarm stopped. The staff laboriously lifted Traylor to his feet and trundled him away.

"Call hospital police," Xiang said. Then he walked into the

nurses' station and clicked on the overhead microphone. "Shakedown, gentlemen, shakedown," he said, then keyed a wall switch and that ungodly electronic shriek ricocheted up and down the hallways. Palanqui called for backup help.

The patients stood frozen in the hallways; then the familiar fandango began. Staff poured out of the nurses' station and wove the men toward their rooms. In succession, as quarters filled, Xiang locked the doors. Then we gathered in front of the nurses' station. Palanqui cut off the alarm.

The unit door split open, and a phalanx of helmeted cops strode down the hallway, the brace of German shepherds with them. Xiang waved them over.

"What have you got?" Bangban said.

"Mr. Traylor is drunk," Xiang answered. "Either pruno or a still."

"Divide up," Bangban called, and everyone split into teams.

The cops unlocked rooms, frisked patients, and turned up bedding, drawers, and laundry. They scoured the bathrooms and closets. Plastic bags began to fill: pills, cigarettes, a crude shank.

After an hour, all the rooms save one had been searched and sealed and the patients led out to the day hall. The final room, again, belonged to McCoy. Xiang unlocked the door. The cops stepped in with the tethered dogs. The staff and I stood behind.

McCoy dispensed with the charm. "You assholes have a warrant?" he hissed. "This is my property. My place." He stood in the middle of the room, arms across his chest.

The cops formed up four abreast. The dogs strained. Bangban slid a truncheon from his belt. "Step aside, Mr. McCoy," he said as the cops edged forward.

McCoy stood his ground. The cops moved closer.

"Fuck all of you," McCoy said finally, and gave way.

A cop stood by McCoy as the shakedown crew set to work. I made myself conspicuously absent, standing out of view on the other side of the doorway.

The staff executed the routine perfectly: McCoy's bed was stripped, mattress tumbled, and drawers emptied. Near a pile of laundry that lay on the closet floor, one dog barked, then both. They dug with their paws.

Two cops pulled the dogs away and Bangban stepped forward. He snapped on a pair of latex gloves, pondered the laundry pile, and then gently peeled down the mound one cloth piece at a time. A shard of metal exposed, Bangban pulled faster until a metal-and-glass apparatus appeared. He reached down and hoisted the prize.

"It's a still," Bangban said.

Xiang walked over, touched the end of a copper tube, and sniffed his finger. "It's the good stuff," he said. "Made with real yeast."

"The hospital never uses yeast for anything," Palanqui said. "It's near the top on the contraband list."

"It always comes in from the outside," Xiang said.

With a pang, I thought of Carstairs being escorted through the halls by McCoy. I imagined there had been payment for that service.

"Let's go," Bangban barked, and guided McCoy toward the door.

McCoy jerked his arm away and headed out. As he went by, McCoy turned, touched two fingers to his lips, and blew me a kiss.

Both search teams gathered at the nurses' station while the police cataloged and photographed each item collected from the search. They took numerous pictures of the small still, an ingenious contraption made from broken cafeteria drinking glasses, metal tubing from a bathroom faucet, and, for a fire pan, a sheet of courtyard window flashing.

The cops bundled up the haul, adjusted their belts, and moved out.

"Where's Carstairs?" I asked.

"She's off for two weeks," Xiang replied.

Traylor sobered up but lay in bed for two days sipping water and taking aspirin. McCoy stayed in his room as well until the dust settled. Then he strolled the halls and held court in the cafeteria as if nothing had happened. He'd taken to sitting with Boudreaux and Mathews. "The Holy Trinity of Trouble," Cohen called them when we'd first noticed the new seating arrangement.

There were no further problems with alcohol. On Friday, talk was all about basketball.

"Good luck to both of you in the game today," Palanqui said to Cohen and me after rounds.

"With Kobe Bryant, you don't need luck," Cohen said.

"We'll all be there," Monabong added. "And the people from Unit B, too."

"Good," Cohen said. "We'll get crushed in front of a crowd."

At quarter to two, my team and I entered the gym. People lined both sides of the court.

The usual pregame routine unfolded. Cohen led Unit B in a cohesive layup-and-shooting drill, while my group casually lobbed a few shots at the hoop, then stood back as Boudreaux executed his leaping, underhand spin move. Even the Unit B players stopped to watch. The trophy was ours.

Halston blew his whistle, assigned each team their respective baskets, and handed a Unit B player the ball. "Play ball," Halston said.

"Game time," I called out, and we were off.

The game proceeded exactly as I'd imagined. Everyone shot whenever they pleased. An occasional ball found the bottom of the net. Unit B passed the ball more than we did. Feet got tangled. But everything came down to Boudreaux. He drained three long jump shots, rebounded four missed attempts by teammates, and easily put the ball back up and in the basket. Near halftime, we led sixteen to four.

Then, after a Unit B missed shot, Caruthers dribbled the ball from their end of the court to ours and passed it to Carver, who handed it to Boudreaux near the free throw line. Boudreaux, as do all clever ball handlers, held the ball behind his hip, leaned toward a defender, faked a dribble to one side, then scooted toward the basket from the other. To the crowd's delight, he again attempted the underhand spin move.

All the players watched, except one. Mike Morgan from Unit B saw where Boudreaux was headed and met him there. As Boudreaux spun, Morgan reached out a hand and batted the ball away. It bounced harmlessly toward the Unit B side of the court.

Boudreaux landed and looked at the rolling ball. He looked at Morgan. His head ticked, his shoulders tightened, and he smashed Morgan in the mouth with his fist. Blood sprayed in an arc.

"Raymond!" I shouted, and stood. Staff and police rushed forward. Xiang pulled an alarm and sirens rang in and outside the gym. Cohen and the cops got to Boudreaux first and managed to bowl him over before he could do more damage. Nurses joined in. The gym doors flew open, and reinforcements arrived.

A dozen cops pushed their way forward and, arms and legs flying, finally subdued Boudreaux. Four officers lay on top as two others bound Boudreaux's arms behind him.

A nurse placed a towel on Morgan's mouth and the Unit B staff assisted him out of harm's way. Cohen, shirt ruffled and face red, huffed beside me. The cops hauled Boudreaux to his feet and jostled him toward the exit.

Stunned, I forgot to move out of the way. "You fucking bloodsucker," Boudreaux screamed as he and the cops passed. Eyes wild, red with rage, he yanked his head to the side and spit on my shirt. "I should have killed your bloodsucking ass when I had the chance," he hissed.

"Didn't you promise to control him?" Halston asked, clearly still upset.

I didn't answer.

How could I have been so dense? I wondered as the gym cleared. Someone could have been killed. And for what? So that I could pretend to be Phil Jackson? Phil Jackson? It was an intramural basketball game between two teams of psychotic convicts at a state mental hospital. "What did you think was going to happen, you moron?" I said to myself out loud.

"How'd the basketball championship go?" John asked at dinner.

"We were way ahead," I said. "Then a player got out of line. Nothing major. But they suspended the game."

"That's unfortunate," Ingrid said. "I know it meant a lot to you."

"It's no big deal," I said.

"You talked about basketball in your sleep last night," Ingrid said.

"I was a little disappointed," I said.

CHAPTER TWENTY-SIX

I carried it too far, that's for sure.

—Jeffrey Dahmer, who raped, murdered, and dismembered seventeen men and boys during the years 1978–1991. On November 28, 1994, he was beaten to death by a fellow inmate at Columbia Correctional Institution in Portage, Wisconsin.

On Monday, the cops went with the staff to see Boudreaux in his room. Owing to the violence of his assault, he'd spent most of the weekend in the seclusion room. But, as was his custom, he'd cleared quickly. That morning he lay in bed reading, but when he saw us he set his book down. I recognized the cover: Salinger's *Catcher in the Rye.*

"Mr. Boudreaux—" Xiang began, but Boudreaux cut him off.

"I'm so glad you came by," he said, and stood. His drawl was a faint whisper. "I feel terrible for the way I acted. They tell me I was a first-class idiot. Please convey my deepest regrets to the poor fellow I hit. And, Dr. Seager, kindly forgive me for my unconscionable disrespect. I'm truly sorry."

"That's okay," I said finally. "We just want to be certain you're not planning to harm anyone else."

"Oh, Christ, no," Boudreaux said, and seemed truly abashed. "I don't know what comes over me. But I understand I'm responsible for what I do. Officers, if you've come to arrest me, I'm fully prepared to face whatever charges await."

Bangban looked confused. "No charges," he said.

"We appreciate the apology, Mr. Boudreaux," Xiang said. "I'm certain it's accepted by Dr. Seager." I nodded. "But you are correct; you are responsible for your conduct. No off-unit activities for one month, including library."

Boudreaux picked up *Catcher* and looked at Xiang. "I'll have this thing memorized in a month," he said. "Holden Caulfield, Phoebe, and the gang at Pencey Prep will get to be my good friends."

MIDWEEK, LEAVING THE unit, I glanced over and saw Cohen canted casually against the door frame of Caruthers's room. Caruthers stood just inside. Engaged in conversation, both suddenly laughed. I'd never seen them speak.

I stopped by Caruthers's room later that day. The staff had all gotten an email regarding three new patients coming to Unit C, one of whom was going to be Caruthers's roommate, replacing Ortega. I wanted to give him a heads-up.

"You'll be getting someone new in your room," I said. We stood in the doorway, as he'd done with Cohen.

Caruthers paused. "I figured," he said. "Any idea who it is?"

"I just have some names," I said. "Ms. Henry will let you know."

"It will be hard," Caruthers said.

"I know it will."

We stood for a long moment. "I saw you speaking with Dr. Cohen this morning," I said finally.

Caruthers brightened. "He saved my life."

"He what?"

"He saved my life," Caruthers said again. "Didn't he tell you?"

"Tell me what?"

Caruthers motioned me inside. I sat in a wooden chair, he on the edge of the bed. "You remember when Manuel died?" Caruthers said.

"I do. And I'm so sorry."

"Thanks," Caruthers said. "Manuel meant the world to me. And I was really troubled after he passed. It was terrible. You were right to be concerned," he went on. "But I lied to you."

"Sorry?" I said.

"You asked if I felt suicidal."

"I remember."

"I said I wasn't. That was the lie."

"What?"

"I did what you asked me to do, though," Caruthers said. "You said if I felt bad to talk to staff."

"I did. You're right."

"I'm ashamed to admit it," Caruthers said, "but I had the razor blade out. My mind wasn't right. I actually made a cut." He turned an arm and showed me a nick inside his wrist. "Then I remembered what you said and I headed to the nurses' station. Dr. Cohen walked by. He saw I was upset and asked if I wanted to talk.

"We went to a side room," Caruthers continued. "And damned if he didn't sit up most of the night with me. The nurses checked in but Cohen just kept saying, 'We're okay.' I don't know what time he left but it was late. And I felt a lot better." Caruthers relaxed. "Didn't he tell you about that?"

"Never mentioned anything," I said.

"Dr. Cohen is the best," Caruthers said.

ON THURSDAY, KATE Henry was late to rounds.

"Sorry," she said, and set a stack of papers on the table, then took her seat.

"The new patients?" Cohen asked.

"They'll be here Monday," Kate Henry said. "We'll go over them at the end."

As we were all anxious about the new arrivals, rounds passed quickly. Finally all eyes turned to Kate Henry, who picked up the top folder and opened it.

"Richard Van Zandt," she said, and the veteran staff members groaned.

"Van Zandt is a re-admit," Kate Henry said. "He was here four or five years ago. We had some difficulties."

"What's he back for?" Palanqui asked.

"Same thing," Kate Henry said. "Lewd and lascivious acts on a child."

"What 'difficulties' did you have?" Cohen asked.

"He gets dirty," Xiang said.

"He'll gas you," Palanqui said.

"I don't think I want to know," I added.

"He throws urine and feces," Xiang explained. "Form of protection. Keep people away."

"No kidding," Cohen said.

"He will take Wilkins's spot," Xiang said. "In with Smith."

Kate Henry opened the second chart. "Hamilton Murbank," she read. "He's older, sixty-two. White. Homeless. I got a call from the jail. They said he's a real live wire. So we'll need to be ready."

"I'll order emergency meds before he arrives," I said. "Just in case."

"Put him in with Caruthers," Xiang said. "He did well with Ortega."

"And finally, DeJuan Newman," Kate Henry said. "Thirty-seven. African-American. Transfer from a state facility in Los Angeles. Assaulted someone in a psych hospital down there."

"Half these guys have assaulted someone here," Cohen said. "Why don't our guys go somewhere else?"

"He must have assaulted someone important," Kate Henry said.

I had an unsettled feeling. "What part of Los Angeles is he from?" I asked, and Kate Henry thumbed through Newman's report.

"Willowbrook," she said.

"That's bad," I said. "Martin Luther King hospital is in Willowbrook, next to Watts. The army sends their trauma surgeons to MLK to learn about gunshot wounds. I did my residency there. Willowbrook is major gang territory. Caruthers is from there as well. There may be bad blood. Have the cops here when Newman arrives."

That done, Kate Henry pushed the report pile aside. "And this brings me to another pleasant subject. We're all aware that the state budget has been in crisis for some years. And up until now, we've been able to avoid serious cuts."

"Until now . . . ?" Cohen asked.

"Dr. Francis has been officially notified," Kate Henry went on. "The budget for every state hospital will be decreased. We don't know by how much. But we will face reductions."

"By reductions," Larsen said, "do you mean layoffs?"

"By reductions, I mean layoffs," Kate Henry said. "They'll be based strictly on seniority, so we don't have much to worry about."

"Except me," I said.

"And me," Cohen added.

"I've been here twenty-five years," Kate Henry said. "They've never laid off a doctor."

"We'll see," Xiang said.

"The first round of letters should go out soon," Kate Henry said. "Then we'll know more."

The next morning, I opened my office door and saw an envelope on the desk. It had no stamp. I pulled out the missive inside. It was printed on official California State letterhead and read: "Owing to budgetary difficulties, your current employment position at Napa State Hospital will be severely impacted. At the close of business on June 1, your services will no longer be required." At the bottom was a stamp of the governor's signature.

I left the letter on my desk, walked over, and stared out the window into the abandoned garden. *I know how you feel, Mr. Garden,* I thought, and smiled to myself. I knew my leaving Gomorrah, reason aside, would make Ingrid and John happy, but still . . . there was a certain insult involved. Who wants to get laid off? Doctors don't get laid off. I hadn't gone to school all those years and worked so hard to get laid off, for Christ's sake. But then again, I thought, no more dodging Mr. McCoy. Or dealing with Cervantes and his stupid eyeglass stems. Or watching my nurses take beatings.

Just then, from over the garden wall, a magnificent teal-and-green peacock fluttered up to the top brick. Sunlight glinting off his splendid fanned tail, he raised his head in a full-throated call, turned, and defecated a load of pellets onto the ground in front of me. I laughed out loud.

Letter in hand, I knocked on Cohen's door.

"Did you get a letter?" I asked.

"Letter? What letter?"

I held up the paper. "I'm getting laid off," I said.

Cohen took the sheet and read it. "Jeez, I'm sorry," he said. "What are you going to do?"

"I haven't the faintest idea," I said.

At home, in the driveway, I read the letter again and the name of my emotion was finally clear: anger.

"I'm getting laid off," I said.

"What?" Ingrid asked. We'd read about the state's fiscal problems and knew of potential layoffs, but it's different when one lands in your lap.

"I got a letter this morning," I said. "They tell me my position will be 'severely impacted.' Severely impacted? They couldn't even use the word *layoff*, for Christ's sake. They said my services would no longer be required at the close of business on June first. When is the 'close of business' in a hospital? What kind of bullshit is this?"

"I'd be angry, too," Ingrid said. "It's disgraceful, and they handled it poorly. You're a physician. I mean, a letter?"

"Does that mean you won't be working at Gomorrah anymore?" John asked.

"That's what it means."

"Cool," John said.

"It does solve a problem," Ingrid added, veering slightly from her strictly supportive stance. "You know Gomorrah frightens us. And I think it frightens you more than you let on."

"I'm not scared," I said and immediately knew that was a lie. "I mean, of course I'm scared sometimes, but not always. And getting laid off doesn't solve problems, it creates them."

"I'll go back to John's question," Ingrid said. "Doesn't this get you out of Gomorrah?"

"Isn't that a good thing, Dad?" John added.

I flashed back to my first day at work, to the arduous trek through the sally port, the dropped keys, the alarm, and the terror of McCoy on a rampage. I thought about Dr. Tom and Cohen and Xiang and Hancock and Caruthers and basketball and lots of things. And still an answer wouldn't come.

That night before we climbed into bed, Ingrid caught me staring out the bedroom window toward the city lights.

"Why can't you let go of that place?" she asked.

We didn't speak any more about the layoff. My family knew I needed time. I mulled over some options as we worked in Ingrid's newly planted vegetable garden on Saturday.

"I suppose I could do locum tenens," I said, and turned a spadeful of dirt.

"Good idea," Ingrid replied, and looked up from her tomato seedlings.

Locum tenens is a well-recognized employment option for physicians. Locum tenens firms contract for temporary jobs in locales nationwide, usually to cover for another doctor on an extended vacation or to fill an unexpected vacancy. A contract may run a few weeks to months. There are lots of positions like this in psychiatry.

"Or there must be other jobs around here," Ingrid continued.

"I'll start looking," I said. Feelings aside, I was going to get laid off, and something had to be done.

CHAPTER TWENTY-SEVEN

You're all trying to figure out what went wrong inside my head. Fucking idiots. You'll never crack the code. . . . You'll never get into my castle. You'll never even get past the gate.

—Brent Runyon, *The Burn Journals*. Runyon, a young adult author and contributor to *This American Life*, set himself on fire at age fourteen.

"You heard Kate Henry, they won't lay off a doctor," Palanqui said at rounds on Monday. "It's hard enough getting you guys to come here in the first place."

"I've already received a letter," I said. "It's a done deal."

"You work for the State of California," Monabong said. "Nothing is ever a done deal. They send out way more letters than people they actually lay off."

"What a stupid way to do business," I said.

"It's California," Cohen added. "We elected the Terminator as governor. Anything is possible."

"They won't lay off a doctor," Palanqui reiterated. "Something will happen."

The remaining staff voiced a similar opinion and we moved on. Xiang went through the black book apace, then turned to Kate Henry.

"Hospital police will be here any minute," Kate Henry said. "Mr. Newman is with them. Dr. Francis put off the other admits until Tuesday and Wednesday."

We walked into the hall and heard keys in the main lock. Escorted by two cops, a tall, thirty-seven-year-old black man strode in with a confident swagger. A six-inch scar ran down his forehead, through his right eyebrow, and over his cheek. He was missing his right eye.

We didn't get a chance to meet Mr. Newman. As Bangban removed Newman's wrist shackles, Caruthers walked in front of the nurses' station and glanced down the hall. "Fuck!" Caruthers shouted, and took off running. Newman lit out behind him. The cops and I sprinted after the thundering pair.

Caruthers skidded into one of the side rooms, slammed the door, and locked it. Newman threw himself against the door.

"You son of a bitch!" Newman screamed and beat the small window with his fists. "I'll kill your fucking ass!"

Xiang pushed his hip alarm, and sirens blared.

SWEATY AND SPENT, Cohen and I leaned against the hallway wall opposite the seclusion room. Inside, Newman pulled so hard against his restraints, the metal bed frame danced along the floor. It sounded like a safe rolling down cement steps. Above that noise, Newman continued to scream. "I'll kill you, Caruthers! I'll fuck you up!"

Palanqui followed Xiang into the restraint room, syringe cocked. After they left, the jostling and shouting gradually faded.

"I'll go check on Mr. Caruthers," I said to Cohen. "You stay here with Newman."

I walked down four doors and entered the side room. Caruthers startled. "I can't be here with him," he said. Sweat sprinkled his forehead. "It can't happen. I'll kill myself first."

"Let me make a call," I said. "I'll see what I can do. I'll be in the nurses' station. Stay here. Keep the door locked."

I called Dr. Francis and explained our dilemma. "We'll get Newman out of there," Dr. Francis said. "I'll see who we can trade on Unit B."

I told the staff to expect a call about a transfer, then I walked back down the hall. By then, Newman was settled down and Caruthers had gathered himself. I entered the side room.

"Newman can't be here," Caruthers said, and his anxiety started to escalate again.

"He's leaving," I said. "Going to Unit B."

Caruthers sighed. "What about the hallways? The cafeteria? He'll get me somewhere."

It was déjà vu. We were back in Los Angeles, where street gangs first festered. Now they'd metastasized, even to Gomorrah.

"Tell me what happened, Tom," I said.

"You knew me back then," Caruthers said. "I'd been off my meds for a while and was flying pretty high. Newman's brother Enos and I got into it over a drug deal or a woman or what exactly I can't recall. But he said something, then I said something. We ended up in front of an abandoned warehouse. Two of us went in, one came out."

I'd forgotten how much Caruthers had changed. But still, that was now two people he'd killed.

"Newman is bad news," Caruthers went on. "He was in prison when he heard about Enos. By the time he got out, I was long gone. But he won't ever forget. He'll shank me for sure."

"We'll protect you," I said, but I wasn't certain I believed it. I heard the cops arrive and escort Newman upstairs. I walked Caruthers back to his room and added "gang hits" to my list of potential problems on Unit C.

Late that afternoon, I collected some charts off my desk, walked to the unit, and headed to the nurses' station, where most of the staff sat. I entered and slid the charts back into their labeled spots in a wall rack.

"Canteen time, gentlemen," Xiang announced over the microphone. "Canteen, gentlemen. Sodas and candy." Each unit at Gomorrah has vending machines locked in a side room. The patients are allowed, twice a day, to access the machines and spend part of the monthly allowance issued to them by the state. It was the one time during the day when you could guarantee patients would be out of their rooms. Larsen supervised the event. She unlocked the side room door.

Amid the hubbub of patients moving toward the vending machines, in a hallway to our left, like a salmon swimming upstream, Burns, head bent, arms pumping his wheelchair madly, zoomed by in the opposite direction. Breaking from the pack, he skidded around a corner, then accelerated down an adjacent hallway, propelling his chair as fast as possible.

The staff followed. We turned the corner just as Mathews sleepily opened his door and stepped out. He hadn't gone two feet before the speeding Burns arrived and rammed his chair into Mathews, who tumbled awkwardly to the ground.

Burns, whom I'd never seen move an inch without his chair, put a hand on either chair arm, pushed himself up, and stood. He reached under a cushion on his chair, slid out a long metal shank, raised it into the air, and tried to stab Mathews in the gut.

Mathews blocked the sharpened pike with his hand and a gush of blood erupted. Burns still within reach, Mathews got his bearings and sprang to his feet. Arms out, he took a step toward Burns and slipped on a patch of blood, falling backward. Unable to soften the blow, his head whammed soundly on the floor.

Burns wheeled around and peeled back down the hallway. Xiang pulled his alarm. "I said I'd get that son of a bitch," Burns said as he pumped off.

We got to Mathews, who groggily pushed Xiang and Cohen aside and struggled to stand. "Fucking asshole, Burns," he bellowed. "I'll knock his fucking head off." He took a few steps, wavered, and slumped to his knees. Red blood oozed from behind his right ear.

We eased Mathews to the floor and Palanqui called the paramedics. After a bit, Mathews settled down and quit trying to stand. The nurses monitored his vital signs while I did a quick neurological evaluation. Within ten minutes, the same group of medics that had attended to Wilkins turned the hall corner.

Mathews roused again after we'd loaded him up. "He fucking shanked me," he moaned, and tried to struggle off the gurney. A medic pushed his shoulders down. "Son of a bitch. I'll fucking kill all of you," Mathews groaned, and the paramedics wheeled him away.

"Don't worry, Doc," a paramedic said. "He's going to make it."

I had mixed feelings.

Hospital police arrived and began a thorough investigation. They took statements from everyone.

"I see you a lot," Levin said to me. "You're just Mr. Magnet for Trouble."

"Excuse me?" I asked. I'd had my fill of Levin.

"I'm sorry," Levin said, and smirked. "I meant you're just *Dr. Magnet for Trouble.*"

I didn't reply. I waited my turn, then told the investigators what I'd seen and done. One cop put yellow tape around Mathews's door. Another cornered Burns and wheeled him away. As Burns passed, the patients in the hallway cheered.

"Have a nice day, Doc," Detective Levin said on his way out.

"You as well," I replied.

As I sat in the nurses' station, I reflected for a moment on Burns. And then I thought about the other older men on the unit. Frail and bent, they were naturally seen as sympathetic and kindly. As most were. Many were the older guys, like Xiang said, who'd come to Gomorrah before the fence went up. But that wasn't the case for all the older guys.

Some of them had committed crimes just as heinous as anyone else's. They were murderers and rapists, too. These old men were no wiser; they'd just lived longer. As Burns had shown, they could shank you just as easily as the younger patients could.

IT'S NOT WELL known, but nonetheless true, that only about one-third of psychotic persons have a mental illness. And less well known still that, motion picture portrayals notwithstanding, mentally ill people don't see things. The next day, our new patient proved it.

The syndrome of psychosis is defined by four symptoms. First is hearing voices. Second is delusional thinking: a delusion is a "belief impervious to reason." Third is a disorder of thought form, when a person's grammar gets scrambled or when made-up words, called "neologisms," are inserted, like calling a table a "zipgel." Making words rhyme incessantly, called "clanging"—"I'm going to the store, more, gore, bore"—is a thought disorder as well. Last is a grab-bag symptom called "bizarre behavior": trying to swim down the street, wearing tinfoil hats, dressing in five overcoats during the summer, that kind of thing.

A person needs only one of these symptoms to be psychotic, but some people have two, and some have them all. They are called "positive" symptoms and attract the most attention from family, passersby, and the police. These are the symptoms ameliorated by antipsychotic medications such as Haldol, Abilify, Zyprexa, Thorazine, and the like.

The second group of potentially psychotic persons suffers from dementia. Dementia comes in many forms, some better known than others. Alzheimer's disease, Lewy body disease, HIV-related, and Huntington's chorea are some of the common types. More recently, vascular dementia, resulting from a series of small strokes, and post-traumatic dementia—brain injury from car accidents, boxing, football, and soccer head trauma—have gained headlines.

Demented people, especially if they become ill, can behave strangely. They can be violent and psychotic.

The final group is people who are physically ill yet display dramatic mental symptoms. People who behave oddly due to a physical illness are suffering from a "delirium."

Delirium is a medical emergency and is most commonly caused by serious infections, acute drug or alcohol withdrawal, a brain tumor, low blood sugar, low blood oxygen, temporal lobe seizures, and psychoactive drug intoxication. Many situations are life-threatening. As any ER physician will attest, the craziest people on earth suffer from acute alcohol or sedative withdrawal, so-called delirium tremens or dt's. Low blood oxygen can be caused by heart attacks, pneumonia, strokes, or a pulmonary embolus, a blood clot in the lungs. The complete list is long and detailed.

There are two symptoms of delirium psychosis that differentiate it from mental illness psychosis. One is the waxing and waning nature of the psychotic symptoms in a delirium. A delirious person may be acutely psychotic for only part of the day, and perfectly clear for the rest of the day. Delirium symptoms are often worse at night, which is called "sundowning." In contrast, the symptoms of psychosis due to mental illness stay fairly stable over time.

A second telltale symptom of a delirium is seeing things. Delirious persons swat the air, see imaginary people, and, historically, are tormented by pink elephants.

A psychiatrist is often called on to correctly diagnose a psychotic person who may suffer from an acute delirium, a dementia, or a schizophrenic psychosis. To complicate matters further, mentally ill persons may also become delirious. And finally, a mentally ill person may become demented and then delirious.

No better example to contrast the practice of modern psychiatry—especially hospital psychiatry—from the commonly held perception of the specialty. An acutely psychotic person needs blood work, complicated scans, X-rays, sophisticated medications, urine specimens, and spinal taps. The psychiatrist must be prepared to captain the medical ship and steer it correctly.

On Tuesday morning, we'd barely had time to sort through feelings about the previous day, when hospital police escorted Hamilton Murbank, a straggly, gray-haired white man, tall and tremulous, onto the unit. As before, we'd just finished rounds.

Two cops locked the unit door, then supported Murbank's

elbows as they walked him toward the nurses' station. The cops spoke with Xiang, removed Murbank's wrist shackles, and signed some forms.

"Good luck, old-timer," one cop said, and left.

Xiang took Murbank to the treatment room, which housed all the blood pressure, IV, and medical equipment for the unit, and sat him on a stool. I walked in to check the initial vital sign readings and chatted briefly with Xiang. When we turned around a moment later, Murbank was gone.

I bolted out the door and nearly bowled over Murbank. He stood in front of the wall directly across the hallway from the treatment room, gesturing excitedly and screaming incoherent gibberish.

"B52," I called to Xiang.

"Got it," Xiang said.

Cohen heard the yelling and ran over. We grappled Mr. Murbank back into the treatment room.

"You climhissonhonor . . ." Murbank yelled as he craned to look back over his shoulder and shook a fist.

Xiang gave Murbank the PRN shot, and after a bit the jabbering slowed. Xiang and I remained in the treatment room.

"Do you know where you are, sir?" I asked Murbank finally.

"Neramhalo," Murbank said.

"Do you know the date today?" I continued.

"May fourteen," Murbank said clearly. Xiang and I looked at each other.

"Who is the president?"

"Barack Obama," Murbank said, and stood. He swatted the air around his head as if fighting off a swarm of bees. "Damn targeeters," he mumbled and sat back down.

"He's not crazy," Xiang said. "He's sick." I was certain Mr. Murbank had a delirium, probably superimposed on a dementia and maybe a mental illness as well.

"I'll call County General," I said.

Dr. Vezo, who'd sewn up my head laceration that first day, called back in ten minutes. I laid out the details of Murbank's case and she concurred, saying it sounded like something serious might be going on, and she agreed to admit him to the hospital. She said they would do all the necessary blood work—so there was no point in sticking the man twice—an MRI, a chest film, and probably a spinal tap as well. We just needed to get him over to County General.

I said we would do that. Then Vezo hesitated. "We saw Mr. Mathews yesterday," she said finally. "The guy your patient stabbed. Are you okay up there?"

"Good as can be expected," I replied.

"I hear you're facing layoffs," Vezo said.

"We are."

"That's rough," Vezo said. "I'm sorry. But hey, maybe you'll get lucky and they'll boot you out."

"Actually, I am getting—" I said when I heard "CODE BLUE ER!" over the phone and Vezo dropped the receiver.

THE NEXT MORNING, we completed the trifecta of new patients when Mr. Van Zandt arrived. He came at the usual time, just after rounds. A burly fist of a man, late forties, white, ridden hard by life, he walked to the nurses' station. held out his arms and Bangban removed the shackles.

Van Zandt rubbed his wrists, put both hands on his hips, and took a look around. "Great to be back," he said.

It took a while to get Van Zandt situated. Xiang took vital signs. I did a quick interview, then went to my office and entered his medication, diet, and general orders into the computer. Later that day, I headed back to the unit to be certain things were settled for the night.

As I unlocked the door, a woman screamed. I sped down the hall. Palanqui ran toward the nurses' station, the front of her smock dripping wet.

"Urine," she moaned. "That asshole, Van Zandt."

Palanqui pushed through the station door and headed to the sink. Monabong dashed over, and Xiang ran out to a laundry cart and grabbed a stack of patient gowns.

I headed to Van Zandt's room and saw that the floor was splattered. A smile on his face, Van Zandt reclined on the bed, hands clasped behind his head. He turned as I walked in.

"I told her not to come in here," he said. "I remember that little Flip from last time. Stupid bitch just won't listen."

THURSDAY CAPPED OUR hectic week when we received from Unit B—in the trade for Newman—Mr. Cameron Parsons, one of Gomorrah's most notorious patients. A decade ago, Parsons gunned down strangers at a local bus stop. "They were part of the Parveen Plot," he'd said at the time. "The ones that came down with Jesus. The ones who must be destroyed."

I interviewed Parsons in the afternoon. He sat on the edge of his bed, I in a chair. He was polite, well-mannered, and intelligent. “It’s a pleasure to meet you,” Parsons said when I introduced myself.

We spent the next ten minutes discussing Parsons’s history: where he was born, how he grew up, schooling, etc. Then we spoke about his time in Gomorrah. “It’s been okay,” Parsons said. “Not ideal. But it’s kept the Parveen People at bay.” He cocked his head and his eyes narrowed. “You’re not one of the Parveen People, are you?”

“No. I just work here,” I said. According to Parsons’s old records, the “Parveen People,” their history, beliefs, and plans, were an elaborately constructed delusional system from which Parson suffered. And upon which he frequently acted, often resulting in violence.

“You better not be Parveen,” he said. “There are ways to find out, you know.”

“Is that a threat?” I said, and rose to my feet.

“Take it however you want,” Parsons said. “You Parveen People must be stopped.” His eyes never wavered. “And as you know, I can do that.”

Parsons stood as well, fronted his shoulders, and didn’t look so small anymore. I hastily excused myself and, looking repeatedly over my shoulder, walked briskly back to the nurses’ station. I thought of my first episode with Boudreaux. I’d made some progress. At least I hadn’t been caught on the wrong side of the room.

CHAPTER TWENTY-EIGHT

But my bones said, "Tyler Clementi dove into the Hudson River convinced he was entirely alone."

My bones said, "Write the poems."

–from "The Madness Vase/The Nutritionist" by Andrea Gibson

With the arrival of three new patients, Unit C was unsettled. At home, things were off kilter as well.

"Have you begun to look for a new job?" Ingrid asked at dinner that Friday.

"I've gone through some journals," I said. "And I searched online. Nothing much so far."

No one spoke.

"I'd really hate to move you guys again if—" I said.

"Don't worry about moving me, Dad," John blurted, then realized he'd cut me off. "Sorry," he added.

". . . if I can help it," I concluded.

Ingrid stood. "Who wants dessert?" she asked.

• • •

ON SATURDAY AFTERNOON Ingrid went into the garage to unpack the last remaining boxes from the move, and John walked to Sean Hansen's house for the afternoon. I went upstairs to renew my job search.

I pecked around the Internet perfunctorily. "Inpatient Psychiatry Position," a website header read. I clicked on the link. "Live and work in paradise," the ad copy began. "Full-time inpatient psychiatry position in Northern California." I checked an attached map. It was in Calistoga, twenty miles away.

I suddenly felt excited. *I'll never have to see McCoy again*, was my first thought, and I was surprised at how relieved I felt. Dealing with McCoy was like handling nitroglycerin. No matter how careful I was, I knew one day it would go off.

In moments of sober reality, I knew that most of the guys on Unit C, and especially people like McCoy, Boudreaux, Van Zandt, Cervantes, and, to some extent, even Caruthers, shared that quality. Regardless of how well you think you know them, no matter what boundaries you imagine have been constructed or ties you've forged, no matter what lie you choose to tell yourself, something eventually goes haywire. They've killed, and I think that changes a person. That's why they have places like Gomorrah. These guys are like human IEDs, and you don't want to be around when they explode.

But you can't live like that forever. So you make up some other story about these guys and about Gomorrah. Something, anything else. Something like: If I left Gomorrah, I would miss Tom Caruthers, and Boudreaux when he wasn't sick, and I already missed Michael Tomlin. And not seeing Cohen, Xiang, and the nurses would be truly difficult.

But the first story was the real story, so I returned to the ad, scanning it with a growing sense of anticipation. The position seemed perfect. I headed down to find Ingrid.

She sat on a stool in a far corner of the garage, two empty moving boxes beside her, crumpled newspapers strewn about the floor and three tall stacks of recently unpacked books at her feet. An unrumpled sheet of newsprint lay flat across her lap. She hadn't heard me enter and noticed only as I approached.

"I didn't hear you," Ingrid said. She looked pale.

"Are you all right?" I asked, and stood beside her.

Looking down, I saw the front page of the local paper. Staring back was the chilling face of Adam Lanza. The paper was dated December 15, 2012.

On the morning of December 14, 2012, in suburban Newtown, Connecticut, twenty-year-old Adam Lanza, a young man with a troubled past and a penchant for guns, shot his mother, Nancy Lanza, fifty-two, four times in the head with a .22 caliber Savage Mark II rifle as she lay in bed. Nancy Lanza, a gun enthusiast, had taken her son Adam to a nearby firing range and taught him to shoot. The rifle belonged to her.

Lanza was dressed in all black clothing, save for a green utility vest, in which he kept extra rounds of ammunition. He wore earplugs, an idea he got from news accounts of mass murderer Richard Farley's 1988 slaughter of seven people at the ESL company headquarters in Sunnyvale, California.

Armed with a Bushmaster XM-15 EZS semiautomatic assault rifle, a Glock 10mm handgun, a Sig Sauer 9mm handgun, and another gun as backup, all also belonging to his mother, Lanza drove to nearby Sandy Hook Elementary, a school he had briefly attended. Blasting his way through a glass front door, he entered a first-grade classroom and opened fire on the women and children within.

Principal Dawn Hochsprung, school psychologist Mary Sherlach, and Vice Principal Natalie Hammond heard the shooting, ran into the classroom, and confronted Lanza. In a burst of fire, Hochsprung and Sherlach were killed. Hammond was shot in the foot, leg, and hand, but managed to crawl to safety behind a door. Substitute teacher Lauren Rousseau attempted to hide her fourteen six-year-olds in a back bathroom. Save one, she and all the children were massacred. Lanza moved to a second first-grade classroom, and murdered six students cowering under their desks; he also shot their teacher, Victoria Leigh Soto, who put her body between the students and Lanza.

Anne Marie Murphy, a teacher's aide for special-needs children, enfolded six-year-old Dylan Hockley in her arms. Both were killed. Teacher's aide Rachel D'Avino, employed at Sandy Hook for one week, died protecting her students as well.

Pausing repeatedly to reload, over a five-minute span, Lanza shot 154 bullets into the children and staff at Sandy Hook. He shot each victim multiple times, hitting six-year-old Noah Pozner with eleven rounds. In total, twenty children and six adults died.

When police arrived, Lanza loaded the 10mm Glock and turned the gun on himself.

The mental condition of Adam Lanza was never conclusively determined. As a child, he'd been diagnosed with sensory processing disorder, a poorly defined condition without scientific backing, and later with Asperger's syndrome, a form of autism. Others speculated that he suffered from paranoid schizophrenia. No medical records were produced.

Lanza left no suicide note and destroyed the hard drive to his personal computer before the shooting rampage. However, a search of the Lanza home and a detailed investigation of his online activities proved revealing.

Lanza obsessively played the online killing game Combat Arms, racking up 4,901 matches with 83,496 kills and 22,725 head shots. He scoured Wikipedia posts concerning mass murderers and corrected even the tiniest errors in the entries. He admitted to a fetish for .32 caliber automatic ammunition.

In Lanza's room, authorities discovered a seven-foot-by-four-foot spreadsheet containing every bit of known information about five hundred mass murders. Covered in nine-point type, it gave minute details about the murderers, their victims, and the kinds of guns used for the killings, down to specific models and serial numbers. The enormous spreadsheet required a special printer to produce. Authorities later speculated that Nancy Lanza knew about the spreadsheet and her son's escalating instability.

Here's what struck me as I stood beside Ingrid: had Adam Lanza lived, he would have come to a place like Gomorrah. And someone like me would have been his doctor. He wasn't that different from some of the patients I had already. If he were my patient, I would now be telling you about how he wasn't really so bad, that he had an encyclopedic mind and was kind to the older patients. How we bumped knuckles in the hall and talked about football.

He'd be on my basketball team, and I'd have given him a nickname. I'd discuss him with Cohen. I'd tell the staff to be careful. I'd get very unsettled when he walked Emily Carstairs down the hall.

And Carstairs would explain why she made allowances for Lanza, like she'd done for McCoy. Just as Lanza's mother had made for him.

We would all say that's just natural. Until there was a scream. An alarm. Until everything blew up in someone's face. I'm constantly trying to find the right way to say this: it's impossible to ignore the humanity of these guys and so easy to deny the violence. And if I think about it for a minute, that's actually what's wrong with Gomorrah and their approach to care for the criminally insane.

Ingrid folded the paper and set it on the workbench beside which she sat.

"I know you work with people like that," she said. "But I try not to obsess about it. I accidentally ran across that picture of James Holmes."

"That's Adam Lanza," I said.

"Who can keep them straight?" Ingrid asked. "Christ, there's a new one every week. And the same crap happens each time. A morbid picture of the shooter appears on the news—never the victims, always the shooter—followed by an emotional call for gun control, then a plea for better mental health treatment, and finally an article explaining the insanity defense. Then nothing. Nothing ever happens."

I CHECKED MY email before heading to the unit on Monday. There was nothing about the layoffs. Then Xiang and Cohen appeared at my door and said that Emily Carstairs was back from vacation. Kate Henry wanted us to meet outside the unit door. My heart sank. I knew what this was about. I'd forgotten about McCoy and the yeast.

In silence we walked down the hallway and turned toward the unit. Outside the door stood Kate Henry in business attire. Beside her was Bangban in full uniform and Detective Levin sporting a gray jacket and dark pants with a dark tie, his silver badge centered squarely on his jacket pocket.

Carstairs knew what was happening the minute she saw us. Kate Henry said we needed to talk about Mr. McCoy, and Carstairs actually looked relieved. We sat in the conference room. After Levin told Carstairs that McCoy had told them everything—"Threw you under the bus" was the term he used—Carstairs freely admitted she brought in the yeast. She said it seemed like a simple favor; then Levin explained that yeast was the key to fermenting alcohol. Xiang added that Unit C was hard enough without drunk psychopaths.

Levin told Carstairs that bringing yeast into the hospital wasn't a crime, but that she would lose her job, and Bangban was ready to escort her off the premises.

"I'm sorry I let you down," Carstairs said as she and the cops stood. "But I'm not sorry to be leaving."

At home that night, I received an unexpected email. "Dr. Seager," it began. "We have reviewed your application for our inpatient psychiatry position and are interested in talking to you further. Please contact us at your earliest convenience." It was signed, "Anthony Rutherford, MD. Good Shepherd Hospital."

I sent a quick reply and copied down their phone number, planning to call first thing in the morning.

"I got a positive response from the new job," I said to Ingrid. "It's at Good Shepherd Hospital in Calistoga. I'll call them tomorrow."

"What are they looking for?"

"Someone to run their inpatient unit."

"Not a forensic unit?"

"No. A regular unit."

"With regular crazy people?" Ingrid asked.

I smiled. "Yes, with regular crazy people."

CHAPTER TWENTY-NINE

If I told you what was really in my head, you'd never let me leave this place.

—Emily Andrews, *The Finer Points of Becoming Machine*

At work the next morning I pulled Rutherford's phone number from my shirt pocket and punched the digits into my desk phone. Dr. Rutherford's secretary, Mary, answered. I told her I was calling about their vacant inpatient psychiatry position, and she knew who I was from my Internet inquiry. She said how delighted they were that I'd called and how anxious Dr. Rutherford was to meet me. We made an appointment for that afternoon at the hospital in Calistoga.

I hung up and glanced at the time. Rounds had already begun. I dashed out, trotted to the unit, and paced briskly to the conference room. I apologized for being late and mentioned my scheduling a job interview. The sigh was palpable.

I glanced around the table.

"Where's Randy?" I asked. "He's always here." His was the only empty chair.

"Don't know," Xiang said, and looked around himself. "He didn't call in."

Xiang's look was met with shrugs. "I'll call his house," Palanqui said. "Maybe he overslept."

And with that, rounds proceeded apace. There was nothing much to report; the evening had been quiet. The day's plans were made and we adjourned. I didn't further mention my appointment in Calistoga.

I saw my patients, wrote some notes, ate lunch with Cohen, and cleaned up my computer work. I told the doctor on Unit B that I was leaving a little early and at three that afternoon, I drove out.

Calistoga, the northern anchor of the Napa Valley, set amid rolling hills and filled with period architecture, was a nineteenth-century gem. Founded by the influential Mormon pioneer Sam Brannan, the resort town featured expensive eateries, plush art galleries, and swanky boutiques lining a main street that once housed dusty saloons, bars, and a railway station. The hospital lay just outside of town on a rise overlooking the long, scenic valley. I parked, then stood for a moment and admired the stunning view.

Dr. Rutherford met me near the front door, and he couldn't have been more pleasant. An erudite, thin man of sixty, he escorted me through a large, modern psychiatric hospital. The nurses' station was awash with blinking computer screens, sparkling sinks, and smiling staff. He talked of world-class local wine, five-star restaurants, 401(k)s, and expansion plans.

Rutherford said they needed a forward thinker, someone with vision, someone who could lead Good Shepherd psychiatry into the future. Someone like me. I was flattered. We talked money, night call, and starting dates. The job sounded great and I said so.

"Do you take forensic patients here?" I asked.

"No," Rutherford said. "That's why we have you good folks at Napa State."

I told Rutherford that I needed to think about it and speak with my wife and that I'd get back to him in a week. He gave me his business card and said to call him personally. I agreed to do that and left.

Nearing my car, I sensed something was missing. I stood again atop the sweeping overlook, and it hit me: it was quiet. I'd been there for two hours and no alarm had sounded.

"How did the interview go?" Ingrid asked when I came home.

"Interview?" I said. "Holy cow, was that today?"

Ingrid knew everything had gone well. "Congratulations," she said. "Tell us all about it over dinner."

After we'd settled down, I described my interview day. "Dr. Rutherford offered me the job," I said at the end. Ingrid and John both perked up.

"Are you going to take it?" Ingrid asked.

"I said I'd call him next week. That I needed to talk with you first."

"It sounds perfect," Ingrid said, and John agreed.

"In a week I'm unemployed," I added.

"So are you going to take the job?" Ingrid repeated.

"Yes," I said. "I think I'm going to take it."

The fact that I was leaving Gomorrah quickly took a backseat to another problem. On Tuesday, Randy wasn't at rounds again. He hadn't answered repeated phone calls, texts, or emails. Wednesday saw no Randy, either. Palanqui drove to his house and knocked on the door. Nothing.

By Friday, there were three empty chairs at the conference room table. Then Kate Henry arrived, followed by Cohen. Taking their seats, they looked somber.

"Randy has been arrested," Kate Henry said. "He won't be coming back."

Palanqui and Monabong both gasped. Larsen was stolid. My heart sank. "What happened?" I asked.

"You remember the cigarette sale you saw last summer?" Cohen asked, and sat forward. "And the one on the day before New Year's Eve that no one was supposed to know about?"

"Of course."

Everyone looked at the empty chair.

"Randy?" I said, stunned.

"Unfortunately, yes," Kate Henry replied.

I felt sick. "He's our best tech," I said. "He's family."

The table was silent.

"Ms. Henry nailed him," Cohen said.

"After you made your formal report," Kate Henry began, "Chief Erickson, Detective Levin, and I discussed the event and proposed a plan. I asked Dr. Cohen if he'd help."

"Word got out that I had a load of cigarettes to move," Cohen said. "Pretty soon I began to get feelers. And one person bit."

"We knew it was someone on the inside," Kate Henry said. "We laid a trap and sprung it."

"I waited at the agreed location," Cohen said. "Detective Levin and Bangban rode backup. A dark blue Acura drove up and parked, and, unfortunately, Randy got out. He had three thousand dollars in his pocket."

"Shit," I said.

"We all feel terrible," Kate Henry said. "But Randy brought cigarettes into the hospital. That's worse than heroin. Who knows how many beatings they caused?"

I thought for a second. "Randy brought the cigarettes in," I said. "But who was he selling them to? Who was the other person behind the unit?"

"We have no idea," Kate Henry said. "Randy wouldn't say."

I remembered back to my conversation with Detective Levin. "It had to be a patient," I said.

"We know," Kate Henry added.

After rounds, I sat with Cohen in the conference room. "Did Levin tell you about the piece of fence with no razor wire?"

"He did," Cohen stated. "And later he found an open basement window behind the unit. It was hidden by weeds. The opening was just big enough for a person to slide through."

"If a patient bought the cigarettes," I said, "he couldn't use a basement window. The basement is locked. Like the unit. You'd need a set of sally port keys."

"And who has sally port keys?" Cohen said.

"Do you think a second staff person was in on this?" I asked. "Opening the basement doors?"

"No other explanation," Cohen said. "Unless a patient has a set of sally port keys."

"Keys would mean access to our offices," I said. "The nurses' station and all the medicines in the med room."

"Don't forget the unit door," Cohen added. "And the main door."

"That could never happen, could it?"

"You've read the emails where someone says they misplaced a set of keys?" Cohen said.

I had. It was a fairly common occurrence. "But they always find them."

"During the time the keys are missing," Cohen said, "imagine someone presses each one into a bar of soap, makes a mold, and someone else walks the molds out through the sally port."

"Then they make replica keys from the molds," I added. "And walk them back in."

"Like your car keys," Cohen said. "If cigarettes go for two hundred dollars a pack, what would a master set of Gomorrah hospital keys bring?"

"Jesus, that's a frightening thought," I said.

"It's more than frightening," Cohen replied. "But not for you."

"Not me?"

"You're leaving, remember?"

We left the conference room, walked out of the unit, and headed down the long outside hallway.

"Then no patient ever went over the fence?" I asked.

"It doesn't look like it," Cohen said.

I thought back to the churning helicopters and how frightened Ingrid and especially John had been that night. I remembered Levin and the endless questions. "Randy got what he deserved," I said.

We walked until we arrived at our offices.

"Being part of an undercover sting," I said and pulled keys from my pocket. "That's heavy-duty. I admire you."

"I love that kind of stuff," Cohen said. "You know that."

I opened my office door. "Levin thought I was mixed up in this, didn't he?" I asked.

"He looked a little disappointed when you didn't get out of the car," Cohen said.

Monday marked the first day of my last week at Gomorrah. Driving to work, I thought about Good Shepherd Hospital and realized a week had passed since I'd spoken with Rutherford. I would call him first thing. I caught a glimpse of myself in the rearview mirror. "You're finally doing something smart," I said.

I opened my office door, picked up the phone, and fished for Rutherford's card in my shirt pocket. I set it on the desk just as an alarm rang. I ran out of my office and headed toward Unit C.

Halfway there, Cohen and a new person blew past me. They flung open the unit door and charged inside, with me following closely behind. In front of the nurses' station, Boudreaux banged on the window, which bowed and flexed, about to shatter.

"You bloodsucking whores!" Boudreaux screamed at the staff. "I'll fucking kill all of you. I'll fuck you up!"

Boudreaux stepped back for one final assault. Cohen looked at the new guy and Xiang, who'd arrived from another hallway. "Let's rock," the new guy said, and the trio executed a perfectly choreographed NFL-linebacker takedown. Two went high, one low, and Boudreaux, like a felled tree, crashed to the floor.

I jumped in and tried to neutralize an arm. The women in the nurses' station ran out and leaped atop the dog pile. The main door burst open, and Unit B people joined the fray as well. "Bloodsucking whores!" Boudreaux continued to bellow over and over.

When the cops arrived, our fight with Boudreaux had become a draw. He couldn't move, but we couldn't leave. Like football referees sorting for a fumble, the cops slowly peeled off one staff member at a time until they could secure a plastic zip line around Boudreaux's wrists.

With a bit more difficulty, they looped and snapped a plastic line around his ankles. "Bloodsucking whores!" Boudreaux screamed.

Palanqui ran up with a filled syringe. Xiang, Cohen, and the new man lay across Boudreaux's chest, and I sat across his legs while Palanqui jabbed the shot into his hip. We stayed at our stations, and in five minutes, Boudreaux's yelling and thrashing had slowed, then stopped. A cop cut the ankle strip, and we helped channel Boudreaux into the restraint room.

Then everyone returned to the nurses' station. Cohen, the new person, and I sat down and caught our breath.

"I'm Dr. Seager," I said to the new man. He was in his late twenties, trim, movie-star handsome.

"Sorry," Cohen jumped in. "This is Dr. Frank M. Will," he said. "A new psychologist. He'll be training with me for a month." He turned to Will. "Dr. Seager is the unit psychiatrist."

We shook hands. "Nice to meet you," I said. "Welcome to Unit C."

"Glad to be here," Will said.

"What's the *M* for?" I asked.

"Mays," Will said.

"As in Willie?"

"Is there another?" Will smiled.

I looked at Cohen. "They're hiring new people and laying off the old ones at the same time?"

Cohen shrugged. "Why does anything happen around here?"

The staff gathered for rounds a little late and a bit winded. Xiang sat at the head of the table, big black book in hand. Cohen and Will came in last. When Will sat down, Palanqui and Monabong drew in a breath.

Introductions were made all around. Will nodded as Xiang

called each name. "This is Mazie Monabong, one of our nurses," Xiang concluded. Monabong smiled and looked at Palanqui. "They finally delivered the eye candy we ordered," she said, and everyone laughed.

We discussed Boudreaux first. "What set him off?" I asked.

Palanqui shook her head. "He wasn't in line for breakfast call," she said. "We were about to close the doors. Mr. Boudreaux never misses breakfast. I went down to see if there was a problem. He took one look at me and started screaming that bloodsucker stuff again. I barely made it back to the nurses' station."

"He had that awful look in his eyes," Monabong said. "The one he gets when he's so crazy."

I knew that look. I'd seen it my first week and at the basketball games.

"What's the matter with that guy?" Will asked.

"Beats the hell out of me," I said.

After rounds, I walked to my office and called Rutherford. He answered on the second ring. I said I'd spoken with my wife, carefully considered his offer, and was delighted to accept it.

"That's great," Rutherford enthused. "I'll have Mary get all the medical staff and credentials forms to you ASAP. They'll go out today."

"That sounds terrific," I said.

"Welcome aboard," Rutherford said.

CHAPTER THIRTY

Even psychopaths have emotions. . . . But then again, maybe they don't.

—Richard Ramirez, known as the "Night Stalker." Ramirez received multiple death sentences for the random murders of thirteen people killed during home invasions in the Greater Los Angeles and San Francisco areas during the 1980s. On June 7, 2013, after twenty-four years in prison, he died from cancer on California's death row.

My last week at Gomorrah passed quietly. It was a time of summing up, cleaning up, and clearing out. I tried to sort through my feelings and emotions, most of which I didn't really understand. The staff, however, true to their Gomorrah roots, went about their business as usual.

At rounds on Tuesday, we began with Boudreaux. He was feeling better. Then Xiang read all the names in succession, comments were made, and that was it.

"They've never laid off a doctor," Monabong reiterated before we finished. "Something will happen."

"I've been offered another job," I said, but Monabong was unfazed.

"Something will happen," she said. Then rounds broke.

"You're getting laid off?" Will asked as he, Cohen, and I walked off the unit.

"I am."

"That must suck," he said.

"Of course it sucks," Cohen interjected.

Will suddenly stopped and whipped an iPhone out of his pocket. "Excuse me," he blurted, "I've got to answer a tweet." He walked away, tweeting as he went.

"Can you tweet from inside the hospital?" I asked.

Cohen stepped after Will.

On Wednesday, I passed McCoy in the hallway. "I hear you're leaving," he said.

"That's right."

"You still owe me for that court thing," he said, and turned toward his room. "New law or not, I'll eventually get released."

I didn't breathe right for a while after that. I'd thought threats from McCoy were something to which I might become accustomed. I figured maybe there would come a day when McCoy would make a threat and I would reply with a skillful verbal retort. Or laugh it off. Or say something therapeutic. But that never happened. In fact, my reactions only got worse over time. I still startle sometimes just thinking about him.

Later, as the Unit C patients filed toward the cafeteria for lunch, Cervantes caught my eye, grinned, and tapped his eyeglasses. As usual, one stem was missing. A Popsicle stick had been taped to the frame and balanced on his ear.

That night during dinner, Ingrid said, "Your credential forms came in the mail today from Good Shepherd."

"That's great," I replied.

"You'll get them right back?" Ingrid asked.

"I will," I said. "Tomorrow." Ingrid smiled.

"Good," John said.

"You know what credential forms are?" I asked John.

"No," John said. "But if Mom's happy, I'm happy."

"TOMORROW IS MY last day at Gomorrah," I said at dinner on Thursday.

"I'm sorry, Dad," John said. "But I'm glad. I know that getting laid off is bad; I understand that. And Mom's right, I know you feel bad. But doesn't getting laid off mean no more Mr. Hell-on-His-Face?"

"How does John know about Mr. McCoy?" I asked Ingrid as we prepared for bed.

"John lives here," Ingrid said. "He knows what goes on."

I didn't sleep well that night. I dreamed that McCoy was standing in our driveway. In his arms, he carried the limp body of a child. I woke in a panic. I knew exactly what the dream meant.

I have always been dogged by anxiety. It's a control thing, I know. Understanding that, however, doesn't help. When I was younger, I kept a lucky rubber band around my wrist for years, from grade school all the way through college. It stopped for a while, but it comes back episodically. Since I started at Gomorrah, it had become part of my life again. The rubber band I wear now is thick and has "Wounded Warrior Project" stamped on it, so no one notices it much. Plus I wear a watch.

I've picked probably the two worst jobs for anxiety. Before becoming a psychiatrist, as I said, I worked for years as an emergency room physician. In addition to re-igniting a long stretch of rubber band wearing, I began to read and re-read the same books.

Late one night, five paramedic units arrived with more than a dozen seriously injured people—I never did count—from a terrible car accident on the freeway not a mile from our door. It was total pandemonium.

We were not a trauma center. Surgeons had to be called in. I was the only doctor in the hospital. For the next hour, three nurses, a handful of technicians, and I scrambled to save everyone. And somehow, amid a jungle of IV lines, dangling chest tubes, scores of empty blood packages, a wall papered with X-rays, and the floor heaped with torn paper and shredded plastic, everyone made it up to surgery.

Exhausted, I sat in the nurses' station adjacent to the cluttered, bloody trauma room and attacked the mountain of paperwork the huge crisis had generated. After a bit, I stretched my back and glanced over my shoulder. That's when I saw the tiny arm.

In the trauma room, beneath a pile of soiled sheets and torn clothing, it dangled over the edge of a counter. I stood and raced over. Hurling off the debris, I saw lying on that counter a little girl who looked to be perhaps five. Serenely waiting her turn to be revived, she'd died. In all the confusion, somehow, she had been forgotten.

I stayed up most of the next night and the one following reading *The White Album* by Joan Didion. For a few nights after that it was Kurt Vonnegut's *Breakfast of Champions.* By the time I quit the ER a year later, in addition to wearing an extra rubber band on my wrist, I'd read both books fifty times. Maybe more.

• • •

MY LAST DAY arrived. Ingrid, John, and the dogs all congregated at the door to send me off.

"Give 'em hell, Dad," John said, and gave me a hug.

Ingrid smiled and hugged me, too. Mulder and Scully wagged their tails.

From my truck, I looked at the house before pulling away. To paraphrase John, my family was happy, so I was happy.

I should have reveled in the moment, but I just drove to work. A one-year Gomorrah veteran, I passed smoothly through the sally port, got my keys, checked my red alarm button, and walked toward Unit C.

Peacocks ambled in the morning sun. To my right, a male bird fanned his tail, angled his head, and let loose a call.

I arrived at the end of the main road, crossed the grass, mounted the small landing, slid my key into the lock, opened the door, and stepped inside the Unit C building.

A siren screamed. People burst into the hallway from office doors and surged this way and that. I turned to run toward the unit, then realized it was my belt alarm that had set off the chaos. Kate Henry sorted through the crowd and stood before me.

"Allow me," she said, and flipped up the red button that I'd apparently somehow pressed.

Rounds proceeded pretty much as they had every morning for the past year. Xiang called each patient's name and gave a short summary of their condition. Today, however, the rest of the staff sat in silence. I didn't speak, because I couldn't.

Will broke the reverie when he blurted something excitedly. Everyone looked and he apologized. Then he pulled an earbud from his right ear. It was connected by a wire to his iPhone. I heard the faint but unmistakable patter of a sports talk-radio show.

When rounds finished, no one stood. Palanqui said she would miss me and everyone else echoed the sentiment. It was an emotional moment. And then, as if all responding to some unspoken cue, we tied up the loose ends.

Palanqui said she'd gotten a call from Dr. Tom's wife, Ellen, who said that she and the kids were moving back to Illinois, where she was from. "She had the baby," Palanqui said, and smiled. "A boy, Tom Junior."

Xiang said that Luella Cortes had one final surgery on her face in March, but then he'd lost contact. After that, he said, when he called the house no one ever answered.

Monabong pulled a postcard from her pocket and passed it around. It was from Virginia Hancock. It said they'd made it to the Philippines and had begun building their school.

I told them that I'd read an email that morning from the neurosurgeon at County General concerning Mr. Mathews. He'd apparently fallen harder than we thought. They'd drained a subdural hematoma—a form of bleeding into the brain—and he was now doing well and would be coming back in a couple of weeks. "Unless we fill the bed," Cohen said, and looked at Kate Henry, who stated she was working on just that.

And that was it. No long good-byes. No pot luck. Everyone wished me well, and then we stood and walked out of the conference room.

I blocked out the rest of the morning to say good-bye to my

patients. I stopped by Smith's room and stuck my head in the door. There was scrambling and the chatter of dice on the floor. Murbank—back from County General and feeling well—and two other older men sat on the edge of a bed. I said I was leaving. Behind the bed, Smith waved an arm.

In the hallway I saw Hong walk into his room with Cervantes, so saying good-bye to him was out. Burns wasn't due back from jail until Monday. Mathews was still at County General, but Chambers, Mathews's roommate, lay in bed. I said it was my last day. "Good luck, Dr. Cohen," he replied, then rolled over and fell back to sleep.

Harlan West was at the dental clinic. Shawn Carver was at school. I stopped Floyd Traylor in the hallway. "Good luck, Coach," he said, and walked on. Parsons and Van Zandt didn't know me from Adam.

I found Boudreaux in the dayroom. Thirty days not yet having passed, he was still reading *Catcher in the Rye.*

"I'll bet you're getting to know that book pretty well," I said.

"Would you like me to quote a passage?" Boudreaux said. "Pick a page, any page."

"Today's my last day," I said. "I wish I could have helped you more. I know there's something we can do for you. I just can't figure out what it is. I'm sorry."

"If you think of it later," Boudreaux said, "text me."

I laughed.

"I tell you what, Doc," Boudreaux said, his drawl returned. "If I ever get well, you come be my guest in New Orleans. We'll do Antoine's on St. Louis Street. It's the oldest restaurant in town. One of the Creole grande dames. We'll have pompano en papillote and oysters Rockefeller. You know they invented that dish there. Named it because of the green sauce. Like the old man's money."

"That sounds great," I replied. "But getting you well comes first."

"It would surely be appreciated," Boudreaux said. "And if you don't like the French fare, we'll hit Johnny's Po-Boys down the street. Get a bag of their oyster specials."

"It's a deal," I said. "Good luck."

"*Bonne chance, mon ami*," Boudreaux said.

And finally I spotted Tom Caruthers.

"Last day?" Caruthers said, beating me to the punch.

"I'm afraid so," I replied. "I came to say good-bye."

A long smile spread across Caruthers's face. "You know better than that, Doc," he said. "For you and me, it's never good-bye. You were there when I was young; you're here now; we'll meet up again somewhere down the line. Hell, why do you think I dragged that Koufax card around? I knew I'd see you again. And I know it now, too.

"And if I start to feel bad," Caruthers said, leaning against the door frame, "I can always get Dr. Cohen to babysit me."

I walked to the unit door and checked my watch. It was eleven o'clock. I headed to my office. The rest of the day I cleaned out my work quarters, scrubbed computer files, deleted an avalanche of saved emails, and stared out the window into the derelict garden.

I had lunch by myself. Cohen and Will were at a Psychology Department meeting. I walked to a 7-Eleven across the street from the hospital campus and bought a prepackaged tuna sandwich, a Diet Coke, a bag of chips, and a copy of the *San Francisco Chronicle*.

I ate, did the crossword puzzle, and solved the daily bridge hand while enjoying one last warm afternoon at a picnic table on the English-garden green.

That afternoon, I said my good-byes to Kate Henry and all the nurses. But they were busy, the visits short. I returned to my office, checked everything one last time, shredded my phone list and copies of court letters, put some personal papers in a folder, took a final look around the room, and left.

I walked the long hallway, exited the main building door, and headed toward the central road. After a dozen steps, I turned and took one last look back. Through a screened courtyard door that looked onto one wing of Unit C patient rooms, I saw Cervantes standing in a window. Paper mask intact, pink ear flags hanging, he stared at me. He was naked. He gave me the finger.

I turned and walked on.

"Heading out?" Cohen asked, appearing from behind.

"One last time," I said, and we stepped down onto the main drive.

I handed in my keys and entered the sally port. The last pod door didn't buzz.

"Thanks, Doc," a voice said over an intercom. A door opened and, in uniform, Officer Cole stepped out.

I hadn't seen Cole since the administrative hearing. "Where have you been?" I asked.

"I got a four-month suspension over that Mathews business," Cole said.

"I'm sorry," I replied. "I didn't know. But I'm glad to see you back."

"It's good to be back," Cole said, and shifted his weight from one foot to the other. "I want to thank you for your support at the hearing," he continued. "It helped me keep my job."

"Officer Cole, you're welcome on my unit anytime," I said.

"I've always got your back, Doc."

Then the pod door buzzed, and I walked out through the gates of Gomorrah.

EPILOGUE

A few days later my phone rang.

"This is Dr. Rutherford's office," Mary said. "We are so sorry, but your credentialing paperwork got hung up somewhere at corporate. We think the problem is finally solved, and the contract is in the mail. In the interim, Dr. Rutherford wanted to speak with you briefly about your salary requirements and ask if you could possibly extend your starting date into August. Could he call you in a few days?"

"Sure, anytime," I said.

I hung up. Five minutes later the phone rang again.

"A psychiatry position has unexpectedly opened up." It was Dr. Francis from Napa State. "Would you consider coming back?"

"I'm sorry," I said. "Did you say I could come back to Napa?"

"A position unexpectedly came open," Dr. Francis reiterated. "We'd love to have you back. We know you have another offer. But would you consider us?"

I told Dr. Francis that I needed a day to think about it, which she said was fine. Hanging up the phone, my head swam. The call was totally out of the blue. I had no idea what to make of it or how I felt. I'd been resigned to leaving, and I thought I had a new contract with a new hospital. I thought I was done with McCoy and Cervantes. Done with all the anxiety and danger. I'd only just begun to relax. But in the Franz Kafka world of Gomorrah, I supposed getting laid off and rehired in the same month made sense somehow. I just couldn't see exactly how.

I called Ingrid and told her what had happened. She asked how I felt and I said I didn't know. I tried to explain things but apparently it didn't come out too clearly. She said we'd talk when she got home. She sounded as befuddled as I felt.

Ingrid arrived home early, bearing food from Bangkok Bistro, our favorite local Thai restaurant. We let things settle while we ate. Mostly made small talk.

Following dinner, I told John and Ingrid, again, the story about how I'd been offered my old job back at Gomorrah. I explained that Good Shepherd was clearly having second thoughts; that it seemed like they didn't have their act together. I quoted my conversation with Mary from Rutherford's office. Ingrid was upset, but more at Good Shepherd's ineptitude than my ambivalence.

John stayed quiet. I knew he didn't want me to go back. Ingrid sipped gently from a glass of merlot. "What do you want to do?" she asked, without looking up.

Combat soldiers, the ones who reenlist, always say they went back because of their friends. Because it's the right thing to do. Because it's where the action is.

I said those same things to Ingrid and John. They said what I suppose all those other families said: "Do what you think is best, and we'll support you."

In the end, I reupped.

The next morning, I called Dr. Francis and said I'd be back.

The contract from Good Shepherd never did arrive.

AFTERWORD

Why They Shoot

In America, we watch deranged people kill classrooms of six-year-olds with military ordinance, gun down movie patrons in their seats, shoot congresspersons in the head, and slaughter defense workers, and, while universally horrified, we wring our hands and issue platitudes about guns and mental illness and slam one another for entrenched beliefs. And nothing changes.

I believe our paralysis concerning guns and mental disease is based on some fundamental misconceptions and gaps in our knowledge that, if addressed properly, might point us in a more productive direction. There are two questions that need to be answered: We need to know from what specific mental illness do most mass murderers suffer? And if identification of these people is possible, how do we keep guns out of their hands?

First, let's look at some basic political positions taken on these issues, then address the errors inherent in them and examine some facts.

In response to the Newtown, Connecticut, Sandy Hook Elementary School shootings, New Hampshire senator Kelly Ayotte, a

Republican, stated, "Given the connections between mass violence and mental illness, improving mental health training for those who work in our schools, communities, and emergency personnel will give them the tools they need to identify warning signs and help individuals get treatment."

Wayne LaPierre, executive vice president of the National Rifle Association (NRA) appeared on *Meet the Press* on September 23, 2013, and said, "The outrage ought to be placed . . . on a criminal justice system . . . that doesn't even enforce the federal gun laws (and we could dramatically cut violence); on a mental health system that is completely broken, or a check system that is a complete joke . . ." Specifically concerning the mentally ill, LaPierre went on, "They need to be committed, is what they need to be, and if they're committed, they're not at the Navy Yard . . ."

The *National Journal*, on September 16, 2013, wrote, "Sen. Dianne Feinstein (D-CA), one of the Senate's leading voices on gun control, called for stricter gun laws in the aftermath of [the] killings at Washington's Navy Yard. . . . Her statement reads in part: 'This is one more event to add to the litany of massacres that occur when a deranged person or grievance killer is able to obtain multiple weapons—including a military-style assault rifle—and kill many people in a short amount of time. When will enough be enough?' "

On January 3, 2014, the *New York Times* stated, "After the [gun control] legislation failed, Mr. Obama vowed to take whatever steps his administration could through executive action. He later issued twenty-five executive orders intended to tighten the rules for gun ownership."

This war of words produces nothing of value and gets us no closer to answering our two questions. The problem with such canned responses is that, while often repeated, they are based on suppositions that simply aren't true.

One such flawed assumption is that people have difficulty obtaining mental health treatment and that identifying mentally ill persons is problematic. Not so. Whenever a mentally ill person commits a mass murder, few people who know them are surprised. The perpetrators have all had contact with the mental health system. They have been identified. And they've been offered "the help they need."

The killers had access to treatment before they became mass murderers. But they refused that treatment, which they are allowed to do. Effective treatment for mental illness is available, but treatment works only if the person actually receives it. Just offering mental health care doesn't count. And as we will discuss below, the persons inclined to psychotic violence don't want treatment, never seek treatment, and actively fight treatment when it's thrust upon them. In short, they may need it, but they won't take it.

Another assumption is that the mental health system needs to lock up more dangerous people. Not so. The California state Superior Court locks up dangerous persons, not the mental health system, and it's often this same court that releases them. Courts have their own criteria for "dangerousness" and "need for treatment." A patient's psychiatrist often has strong disagreements with a court decision.

Third, some assume that all mentally ill people are dangerous. Also not so. In fact, persons with mental illness are far more likely to be the victims of violence than the perpetrators. However, some people with mental illness are violent. And the key is to sort those people out from the others.

A fourth common assumption is that criminal background checks will keep potentially violent mentally ill persons from purchasing weapons. Not so. Very few mentally ill persons are criminals. Between 1998 and 2009, 95 million potential US gun buyers' records were checked, and 0.03 percent were declined due to a history of mental illness. Almost all the guns used in American mass murders were purchased legally.

If lots of people are mentally ill, and the great majority are not violent, who then should we be worried about? On the psychiatric spectrum of disease, where exactly do mass murderers come from? Or, just as important, where don't they come from?

They aren't autistic. They don't have OCD. They don't have PTSD. They don't have anxiety disorders, social phobia, or sensory processing disorder.

Depressed people commit suicide, not mass murder. Bipolar manic people tend to be the victims of crimes—again, not the perpetrators. They frighten people. They are often the ones shot by police. And the foil-hat-wearing, babbling street schizophrenic is too disorganized to pull off a carefully planned massacre.

So what's left? The first troubling group is labeled "personality disorders." A personality disorder is a persistently dysfunctional method of behavior that doesn't involve psychosis. The most severe personality disorders carry names like antisocial (sociopaths), narcissistic, and borderline.

While persons with personality disorders commit many crimes, including grisly murders, their behavior and motives can be understood. These people commit crimes of passion: anger, jealousy, revenge, rage. Their murders often involve family members, spouses, or coworkers.

Their crimes may be memorable, but personality disordered people don't commit mass murder.

This leaves one final group. And this group commits nearly all mass murders. They are the group that kills strangers, politicians, schoolchildren, theatergoers, and defense workers. They kill because they have a specific kind of mental illness. I have found that mass murderers are nearly always paranoid.

Paranoid people, usually labeled schizophrenic, may become deeply, profoundly, and fixedly delusional, but unlike most other schizophrenics—the tin-hat people—they remain organized, a fact known for centuries. They retain the ability to function, work, handle money, and plan. They can fill out government forms, amass an arsenal, produce elaborate computer spreadsheets, and implement massacres.

All paranoid persons exhibit a hallmark dysfunction, a symptom called "anosognosia," a Greek term meaning "lack of awareness" or "denial of illness." To a person, paranoid people don't think they're sick, and they cannot be convinced otherwise.

As well, paranoid people have a severely distorted view of the outside world. They universally externalize blame: "I'm not my fault, it's them." In an equally twisted bit of pathology, paranoid persons believe themselves to be the true victims of their conspiratorial beliefs and their actions, even of their horrendous crimes. The refrain is this: "It's not my fault. Look what they (the victims) made me do."

And, oddly, paranoid persons frequently display the flip side of paranoia: grandiosity. Thus they present a disturbing paradox. They say, "The government is out to get me. But I am an omnipotent god. I don't deserve this. That makes me the real victim here. Someone must pay." This is the reason for their committing massacres.

If mass murder is ever to be dealt with effectively, we must develop a plan for these profoundly paranoid but functional people. People who deny they're sick; people who never seek treatment, no matter how much is offered. People who adamantly resist any type of medication or therapy. People who blame society for their troubles, believing—regardless of the horror they've created—that they are the true victims and that the actual victims, the massacred, "got what they deserved."

If mass murder is to be prevented, any identification, detention, intervention, and treatment scheme must be aimed specifically at this paranoid group. New gun laws should focus on them, as well. I have no idea what form that identification, detention, intervention, or treatment may take, or what a proposed gun restriction statute might involve, but I agree with William Saletan, who wrote in the April 7, 2013, *Buffalo News*, "Disclosing mental health problems makes all of us uneasy. We don't want to live in a country where every therapy session is public information. Many of us don't want to live in a country where guns are confiscated over gossip. I can't tell you how to link weapon sales to behavior assessment in a way that avoids these scenarios. But I can tell you this: until we do, there will be more carnage."

AT THE BEGINNING of this book, in the Author's Note, I said that state forensic mental hospitals like Napa State Hospital are not safe. I hope this point has been demonstrated adequately. But to portray the violence is only half the story. The other question now becomes: What to do about it?

Clearly changes are necessary. But what would that change look like? For Napa State Hospital and the two hundred other facilities around the country that house forensic patients, the first step is mandated patient treatment. If someone avoids jail because they're sick, they should have to take treatment to make them well. And that means medication. More medication equals fewer assaults, fewer deaths, fewer problems, and a safer atmosphere for everyone. Sick people don't magically become competent and not insane, but they do assault and kill people.

Second, we need either prison guards or a law enforcement presence on every state hospital unit, and the units need to be configured from a penal model. Either this or certain units need to be designated as "intensive care units," where the ten percent of patients who commit ninety percent of the assaults can be segregated.

For the difficulty faced on just this one issue, let an example suffice. When the idea of these so-called intensive care units was proposed at the state capital, disability rights attorneys objected. The proposed plan called for each patient to have their own room. The attorneys argued that this would be too isolating. At Napa State Hospital, the single most frequent request from the patients themselves is to have their own rooms.

Third, change will be required of the psychiatrists, psychologists, psychiatric nurses, and staff. You are the ones being hit. Say something. Do something.

Fourth, the families of the patients need to be educated. It is your sons, daughters, fathers, and mothers who are being maimed and killed. Say something. Do something.

Up to this point, the state government in California, and no doubt other states as well, has been able to successfully dodge blame for this epidemic of hospital violence. Our governor, currently Jerry Brown, is ultimately responsible for the mayhem committed in the state facilities that he oversees. Write him a letter. Make a call. Make your feelings known.

And we as citizens are all responsible for the carnage wrought in our names, at facilities in our states, to our friends and families. Vote for persons who will bring change.

ACKNOWLEDGMENTS

To my father, Floyd W. Seager, and his sisters, Fay Seager Hanson and Verla Seager Berglund, from whom I learned the art of a story well told. During my childhood, regardless of the occasion, my father and two aunts would take turns telling stories of their childhood during the Great Depression. In later years the stories involved my father's service in the Korean War—he ran a MASH unit and won the Silver Star—his tales of medical practice à la Lewis Thomas, and, toward the end, the rare illness that would take his life. As well, they detailed my aunt Fay's battle with cancer and my aunt Verla's good cheer in the face of declining health.

My father and aunts are gone now, but the wisdom, humor, and courage they displayed is not. Nor are the lessons they taught, the most important of which was humor. I hope I have done their memory proud in telling this story.

This book belongs to my wife. Among her many skills, she is a peerless editor and critic. Any concision, style points, or clarity found in my writing style is due primarily to her. But even more important is the love, partnership, and kindness she demonstrates on a daily basis. I love you. Without you, there would be no book.

As any writer knows, the world is divided into two groups: those with a literary agent and those without. The gulf between these poles is wide and seemingly impassable. To my agent, Jessica Papin, I owe passage from one side of that gulf to the other. Jessica, without your enthusiasm, tireless work, editorial skills, expert advice, and professional, steady hand, this book would never have been possible.

A special thanks to my first agent, Lisa Collier Cool, herself a successful writer. Your help was greatly appreciated and is never to be forgotten. To my brother-in-law, Michael Vezo, with loving memories of my sister, Nancy, six years ago passed. And to my late mother, Beth Anne, you were loved most of all.

To my good friends Ben Levin and Will Cirimele. Thanks for your support and advice and the precious gift of your time.

Many thanks to Caty Becker, Stephanie Evans, and the entire editorial staff at Gallery Books for their much-appreciated expertise and time. Thanks to Mary McCue, Senior Publicity Manager, and Senior Editor Jeremie Ruby-Strauss.

But the most special thanks goes to my trusty editor, Kiele Raymond. What a gem. A finer, brighter, more incisive mind would be impossible to find. There are big things in your future. Thank you.

And finally, to those with whom I work. In the book, a much-loved nurse, Virginia Hancock, retires. She leaves with these words: "May God bless all who live and work within these walls." To everyone at Napa State Hospital, I wish you the same.